To Kim,

For all your devoted
efforts that I have benefitted
the children of our school.
Thank you,
Colleen Besman
& her exceptional
Students

FOOD & SOUL

FOOD & SOUL

EASY & TASTY VEGETARIAN COOKERY

BRAHMA KUMARIS

Health Communications, Inc.
Deerfield Beach, Florida

www.bci-online.com

COOKBOOK COMPILED BY THE BRAHMA KUMARIS, LONDON

ABOUT THE BRAHMA KUMARIS WORLD SPIRITUAL UNIVERSITY
The Brahma Kumaris World Spiritual University is an international organisation working at all levels of society for positive change. Established in 1937, it now carries out a wide range of educational programmes for the development of human and spiritual values throughout its 4,000 centres in over seventy countries. The University is a non-governmental organisation in general consultative status with the Economic and Social Council of the United Nations and in consultative status with UNICEF. It is also the recipient of seven UN Peace Messenger awards. www.bkwsu.com

Library of Congress Cataloging-in-Publication Data
Kumaris, Brahma.
    Food & soul : easy & tasty vegetarian cookery / Brahma Kumaris.
        p.   cm.
    Includes index.
    ISBN 1-55874-948-9
        1. Vegetarian cookery. I. Title: Food and soul. II. Title

    TX837.K79 2001
    641.5'636—dc21

                                                                    2001046335

©2001 Brahma Kumaris

ISBN 1-55874-948-9

HCI, its Logos and Marks are trademarks of Health Communications, Inc.

Publisher: Health Communications, Inc.
            3201 S.W. 15th Street
            Deerfield Beach, FL 33442-8190

CONTENTS

INTRODUCTION

We have corn,
we have apples bending down the branches with their weight,
and grapes swelling on the vines.
There are sweet-flavoured herbs,
and vegetables which can be cooked and softened over the fire,
nor are you denied milk or thyme-scented honey.
The earth affords a lavish supply of riches.

Pythagoras

A DIET FOR THE 21ST CENTURY

As we head into the 21st century, vegetarianism is becoming an increasingly familiar part of daily life around the world. Most restaurants now have vegetarian items on the menu and a passenger can request an airline to provide a vegetarian meal. Supermarkets and other businesses are responding to consumers' demands and bringing out new ranges of tasty vegetarian foodstuffs. More and more people are choosing to become vegetarians, not just on the basis of traditional religious dictates, but out of ethical, ecological and health concerns.

Vegetarianism is nothing new – it's been around in various forms and for various reasons for many, many centuries, but its recent growth is one of the most significant changes in eating habits over the past two or three decades. Young people everywhere, with a love and respect for all life forms, are switching towards a vegetarian diet every day. Their families and friends often begin to follow suit, and feel better for it too.

In fact, a vegetarian diet makes sense in a lot of ways. Moral, religious, health, ecological and economic reasons have motivated vegetarians over the years, and they are increasingly relevant, looking at the strain on natural resources, a variety of meat, poultry and fish-related food scares, a general concern for healthy living and a popular conscience that rejects the unnecessary suffering of animals.

With ever-greater awareness of the need to preserve natural resources and conserve the environment, people are also realising that it makes more sense to eat low on the food chain, closer to the first level of plant protein—legumes, whole grains and nuts. With so many people in the world suffering from hunger and inadequate water, a more efficient use of food resources is to grow crops that feed people directly, rather than use vast amounts of water and agricultural land for grain to feed and raise animals, which then become a small amount of animal protein on a minority of people's plates.

And if you are looking to be healthy and live longer, a vegetarian diet, especially one with a light dairy content, provides a lower or negligible intake of unhealthy cholesterol and saturated fat. Fresh vegetables, fruit and the consumption of whole grains and legumes ensure that there are plenty of vitamins, antioxidants and fibre in one's diet. High and unhealthy levels of salt, sugar, chemicals and hidden fats in processed foods are avoided. Food is digested and passes through the system more easily, which helps prevent any toxic build-up and leaves the individual feeling lighter and fresher. Nutritional studies confirm that vegetarians are healthier and less prone to heart disease, high blood pressure, cancer, diet-related diabetes, obesity, arthritis, rheumatism, constipation, kidney disease and, of course, food poisoning.

Whatever the reason, a vegetarian is a person who has thought about what they are eating.

THREE KINDS OF VEGETARIANS

Along with the growth in vegetarianism, it's also easy to note that people eating a variety of different diets describe themselves as vegetarian. Vegans have the most restrictive diet, excluding not only meat, fish and other flesh but also eggs, milk and dairy products. The lacto-vegetarian eats all dairy products but not eggs, whilst the lacto-ovo-vegetarian supplements the vegan diet with milk, dairy products and eggs. All types of vegetarians exclude animal by-products such as gelatine and animal fat. The recipes in this cookbook are suitable for a lacto-vegetarian diet and include a variety of the nourishing and tasty vegetables, fruits, grains, pulses, nuts and seeds with which today's vegetarian pantry overflows.

GOOD NUTRITION AND PROTEIN IN THE VEGETARIAN DIET

So if there are many very good reasons to be vegetarian, whether for the benefit of oneself, nature or other people the world over, are there any good reasons not to be vegetarian? The myth that a vegetarian diet is devoid of protein or other essential nutrients has long been exploded and the health and nutritional benefits of such a diet now widely accepted. Whilst it is easier to create nutritionally complete meals in a lacto-ovo-vegetarian diet than in the more restrictive vegan diet, judicious planning of the correct combination of vegetarian food for each meal will ensure sufficient protein, minerals and vitamins for all vegetarians. Nevertheless, a popular misconception still seems to be that a vegetarian diet will not provide sufficient protein. Protein can often be found in higher concentrations in non-animal sources. Nuts, such as walnuts and almonds, and legumes, such as peanuts, have a higher proportion of protein than beef. Over the last twenty years or so the recommended daily intake of protein has been reduced to about half and, for those of us not facing hunger, the problem is more likely to be too much protein rather than not enough. More details on protein appear in Useful Information to follow. As long as a diet includes a variety of grains, beans, pulses, nuts, seeds, vegetables, fruit and other produce, with or without milk and dairy products, it will provide all the necessary nutrients. Whilst people may cite taste as a reason for not being vegetarian, there are countless books available nowadays with delicious vegetarian recipes, including this one!

THE SPIRITUAL ELEMENT

"As a person eats, so he thinks.
As a person thinks, so he acts.
As a person acts, so he is."

This book of recipes has been prepared by the Brahma Kumaris World Spiritual University, which encourages individuals to take a more spiritual approach to all aspects of life. In common with our great spiritual, religious and wisdom traditions, the University places great importance on food. Whilst modern science tends to take a technician's approach and see the molecules, chemical compounds and nutrients that feed the body, a more spiritual, holistic perspective also places a sacred significance on what we eat, seeing how its energy can touch, heal and sustain the soul as well. The body needs sustenance, but so does the soul; we must absorb, assimilate and integrate spiritual energy as well as physical. Practitioners of the Raja Yoga meditation, which the University teaches, are typically lacto-vegetarians. They believe that non-violence is an essential characteristic of the spiritually-awakened individual and that the essence of the human soul is peace, tranquillity and love. If the internal workings of the soul are disturbed, then meditative serenity eludes the individual. The meditator sees that whatever food is eaten has an effect on the mind, in a subtle form of the way in which alcohol or intoxicating drugs can dramatically alter mood and judgment.

When a person becomes more aware of the spiritual aspect of his or her identity, the relationship between body and soul takes on a new meaning and greater importance. The awakened inner eye of the soul gives birth to a higher sensitivity and greater awareness, revealing aspects that were previously unfelt or unknown. Subtle energies become very real and the individual is able to perceive very clearly whether something taken into the body is conducive to or inconsistent with the overall well-being of body and soul, intuitively preferring what is right.

With this perspective, food may then be placed in one of three categories. Pure (or 'sattwic') food constitutes the staples of a yogic diet. It includes

fruit, grains, beans, seeds, sprouts, most vegetables, dairy products and a moderate amount of spices and herbs. Then there is stimulating (or 'rajsic') food, which may be consumed in moderation, and includes coffee, tea, colas, vinegar, radishes, spices and watermelon. Finally there are impure (or 'tamsic') items, such as tobacco, alcohol, nonprescription drugs, all meat, fish, fowl, eggs, stale food and also garlic, onions and chives. These should all be completely avoided. Ordinarily onions and garlic are recommended to non-vegetarians as blood purifiers and to help counteract the build-up of harmful animal fat and cholesterol. However, the healthy vegetarian is not in need of such protection and the spiritually perceptive meditator will be aware that they tend to arouse anxiety and irritation – passions which retard serenity and peace of mind. The purer one's diet, the more the emotions remain in a state of equilibrium, bringing tranquillity to the consciousness and greater clarity to the mind and intellect.

CONSCIOUSNESS IN THE KITCHEN—COOKING WITH LOVE!

In today's information age, we are continually bombarded with details about the physical aspects of what we eat and the effects that different ingredients may or may not have, and naturally this is important. But in this welter of information, we tend to overlook one crucial factor: the consciousness of the person cooking and the effect that this will have upon the food, and thus also on those who eat it. A cook prepares food in a physical place, but also in a spiritual or inner space. And just as the physical surroundings are best kept clean and in order, so should be the state of mind of those in the kitchen. A simple and familiar example of this concept at work can be seen in the way that home cooking, especially that of one's mother, holds a special place in our hearts. The love and care with which it is prepared more than makes up for the greater technical skills that may perhaps be found in a restaurant setting where stress, arrogance and greed may flavour the dish of the day.

When this subtle, spiritual aspect is taken into consideration, the role of the cook extends from simply creating tasty, nourishing meals with fresh ingredients, to including a spiritual connection with those who will be eating that food. The aim will be to touch and fill the heart as well as the palate and stomach. The love of the cook, and his or her motivation to offer sustenance, will nourish as much as the chemical components of each dish. Food cooked by a person who is angry, depressed or full of arrogance or hatred will have a

different effect from food cooked with feelings of love, peace and the pure desire to serve. In other words, we are what we eat but also the thoughts and attitudes that have gone into what we are eating. Even in today's demanding society, when there sometimes seems to be hardly enough time to cook, let alone do so peacefully and caringly, it is therefore definitely beneficial to develop a positive attitude towards cooking. Before undertaking any food preparation, remind yourself that the project at hand can and should be an enjoyable, creative activity, rather than an unpleasant, time-consuming chore. A good practice, then, is to meditate before cooking and then to let preparing the meal itself be a creative, meditative experience which yields a balanced, health-promoting diet for the body as a temple for the soul. Food always tastes better when it has been flavoured with love and happiness.

Having prepared food with this attention, Brahma Kumaris' practice is then to offer the freshly-prepared meal to the Supreme. Expressing gratitude in this way serves to enhance the spiritual quality of the food and deepen the individual's personal relationship with the Divine, while also creating a powerful, shared spiritual experience. On a very practical level, it will also help the body to prepare itself to receive and digest food. Of course, the last step is to eat, and this, too, is best done in a peaceful, unhurried and harmonious state of mind and environment; we are what we eat and also how we eat.

The information in this cookbook does not pretend to be a complete guide to nutrition or vegetarianism, which would be beyond its scope. However, whether you are a new, aspiring, partial or confirmed vegetarian, we hope that this book, with its emphasis on the soul as well as the body, will bring an added dimension to your kitchen and dining table. Cooking, and eating, should be a joyful and significant experience. So look, cook and enjoy!

USEFUL INFORMATION

Our overall state of health, well-being and development depends, to a large extent, on maintaining a well-balanced, nutritious diet. The following contains some general guidelines for nutrition and a list of sources from which you can obtain the basic daily requirements. Once you become familiar with the basic ingredients in a vegetarian diet, it is easy to maintain good nutrition whilst also enjoying a variety of tasty meals.

The key areas are protein, B vitamins and iron, all of which will normally be present in adequate quantities in a good balanced vegetarian diet and, whilst attention should therefore be paid to them, they should not be any cause for concern.

Protein

Proteins are made up of chains of basic units called amino acids, which are used by the body as a form of structural material rather than a fuel. The body uses some twenty different amino acids to make the protein it needs. Nine of these are called essential amino acids, because they must be supplied in the food we eat, whilst the rest can be synthesised by the body. It is true that plant protein does not contain all nine essential amino acids. However it is easy to make up the complete balance of amino acids by eating appropriate combinations of food—a process known as protein complementing. This is how it works. To make a complete protein diet, combine, not necessarily in the same meal, legumes with grains or dairy products, or grains with dairy products, or nuts and seeds with green vegetables and grains or legumes. A plant protein, such as a grain combined with a pulse, will yield a high quality protein that is in some cases better than protein from an animal source. Whilst this may sound like something new, many such combinations are already within most people's diet, for example beans on toast, muesli with milk or soya milk, beans or pulses with rice or noodles with beancurd.

Legumes or pulses are dried peas, beans and lentils. This includes all soya bean products such as tempeh, tofu, soya cheese and textured vegetable protein (T.V.P.); in fact, soya by itself is a high quality protein. Grains run the gamut from barley, corn, millet, wheat, oats and rye to rice. Nuts include the familiar almonds, chestnuts, peanuts, pecans, pine nuts and walnuts while the main seeds are linseeds from the flax plant, poppy seeds, sesame seeds and sunflower seeds.

VITAMINS

Whilst important nutrients such as calcium and iodine are often supplied through milk, vegetarians with little or no dairy produce in their diet should pay attention to vitamins D and B_{12}. Vitamin D is synthesised by the skin when in sunlight and is also present in dates, green leafy vegetables grown in the sun and in small amounts in fruits. However, vitamin B_{12}—of which only a very tiny amount is required—is believed not to be available from plant foods (apart from comfrey) and so a good vegan diet will sensibly include food products such as soya milks, dried soya mixes, yeast extract or breakfast cereals that have been fortified with it. However, both of these vitamins are supplied in milk and dairy produce and so in a balanced lacto-vegetarian diet this need not be a concern.

Dates are rich in many minerals and are also particularly valuable for their high vitamin A and D content.

Black currants, citrus fruits, tomatoes and green vegetables are particularly rich in vitamin C, while vegetables in general are a very good source of a variety of minerals and vitamins.

IRON

Iron is present in dried fruits, particularly in raisins, and in certain vegetables, particularly spinach, beetroot, watercress and other green leafy vegetables. Molasses (crude sugar cane juice) and black treacle are also rich in iron. Brewer's yeast is rich in B vitamins, calcium and iron.

GRAINS OR CEREALS

Grains, also known as cereals, include rice, oats, wheat, couscous, millet and buckwheat and are the staple of practically any diet as they provide the body's basic fuel. All these cereals are a good source of complex carbohydrates and can be combined with pulses, nuts and cheese, as explained to provide a complete protein intake.

Whole grain cereals contain all three parts of a cereal grain. The germ or inner part is the embryo from which shoots and roots emerge and contains protein, oils, thiamin and vitamin E. The endosperm, which surrounds the germ, contains carbohydrate and protein. The outer protective husk, from which bran is extracted, is abundant in B vitamins and minerals. Whole grain products are nutritionally preferable to a refined white cereal, the majority of which is derived from the endosperm alone.

1. **Buckwheat** - is not a grain at all, but a fruit seed of a relative of rhubarb. Unroasted buckwheat has a mild flavour. Roast buckwheat dry or sauté in a little oil for a nutty flavour. Cook 1 part of buckwheat with 3 parts of boiling water for 15-20 minutes. Buckwheat is rich in amino acids, calcium, vitamin B and vitamin E, and is gluten-free.

2. **Buckwheat, roasted** - is called Kasha. It has a stronger flavour and is drier than unroasted buckwheat. Cook 1 part of buckwheat with 2 parts of boiling water for 15-20 minutes.

3. **Bulgur Wheat** - is also known as cracked wheat. Soak in boiling water until all the water is absorbed. Cook 1 part of bulgur with 2 parts of boiling water for 15-20 minutes. It can also be cooked with rice.

4. **Couscous** - is the traditional basic dish of the North African countries. It is made from semolina and looks a bit similar to buckwheat. Soak 1 part of couscous with 1½ parts of boiling water. Cover and leave for 10-15 minutes. It is then ready. It can also be steamed over vegetables.

5. **Millet** - is said to be the first grain cultivated by humanity. Before rice appeared, it was the staple food of China and it makes a very pleasant change from rice or other cereals. Cook 1 part of millet with 3 parts of cold water, bring to the boil, cover and simmer for 15 minutes. Allow to stand for 20 minutes. Millet is considered a high quality protein, alkaline, rich in lysine, high in vitamin B and gluten-free.

6. **Oats** - are famous as a breakfast meal. Cook 1 part of oats with 3 parts of boiling water, simmer for 20-30 minutes. Oats are high in vitamin B, high quality protein and minerals, and oat bran helps to lower cholesterol.

7. *Rice, White Basmati* – Wash and rinse the rice well. Cook 1 part rice with 2 parts of cold water, with a teaspoon of salt if desired. Bring to the boil, cover with a tight fitting lid and simmer for 15–20 minutes. There is no need to stir rice or keep removing the lid. Test with the fingertips—when it breaks, it is cooked. Drain and rinse with cold water, or the rice will continue cooking.

8. *Rice, Brown* – Cook as above. Some brown rice may take more water and a longer time to cook. Brown rice contains important nutrients that are missing from milled, white rice.

9. *Rice, Short Grain White* – Cook as above. This type of rice is suitable for making rice puddings.

10. *Spelt* – has been grown and eaten around the world for thousands of years. It is an unhybridised bread wheat. It contains B vitamins, magnesium and more protein than wheat. It can be tolerated by many people who are wheat intolerant and is suitable for making bread, as it contains gluten.

11. *Wheat* – is in the staple diet of at least half the countries of the world. Wheat flour is used for cakes, biscuits, breads, puddings, etc. Hard wheat from the USA and Canada is usually used for breads because it is very high in gluten. Durum wheat, another hard wheat, is used for pasta. Soft wheat is used for cakes and biscuits.

12. *Wheat Berries* – are very tasty with a lovely nutty flavour. Rinse well, put 1 part of wheat berries with 4 parts of water, bring to the boil, cover and cook for 60 minutes until the grains burst and are soft.

LEGUMES OR PULSES (DRIED BEANS, PEAS AND LENTILS)

Legumes or pulses provide high quality plant protein and fibre, have no cholesterol and are low in fat. They contain important B vitamins, many minerals such as calcium, potassium and phosphorus, iron and some also contain vitamin C. To make a complete protein, that is one providing all the essential amino acids, combine legumes with other foods, as explained earlier.

1. *Adzuki Beans* – are reddish brown round beans with a pleasant sweet flavour. They are rich in protein and are known as the 'king of beans' by the Japanese. Soak overnight then cook for at least an hour.

2. Black-Eyed Beans – are beige colored with a black spot or black eye. They cook quickly and have a pleasant taste. They do not need to be soaked overnight. They are native to Africa, but are now grown in India and China. Cook for 30 minutes.

3. Butter Beans – are large, flattish, kidney bean shaped and creamy white in colour. They make good patés and soups. They are a native of tropical America, but are now grown in many countries. Soak for 6-8 hours or overnight. Drain, rinse and cook in fresh water for approximately 45-50 minutes.

4. Cannellini Beans – are white kidney shaped beans from the red kidney bean family. They have a slightly nutty flavour and are grown in Argentina. Soak overnight and cook for at least an hour.

5. Chick Peas – (or Garbanzos) look like small hazelnuts with a light golden color. They taste delicious and can be used in salads and casseroles. They are the main ingredient in hummus. This bean is native to the Mediterranean.

6. Flageolet Beans – are an attractive pale green colour, very slim with a delicate flavour. They are lovely for salads and soups and are grown in France and Italy. Soak overnight and cook for 30-60 minutes.

7. Haricot Beans – are small, oval, white beans which belong to the kidney bean family. These are the beans used in 'Baked Beans' and also flans and salads. They have a slightly sweet flavor. Soak overnight and cook for 1-2 hours.

8. Kidney Beans – red or black, have a very rich flavour and kidney shape. They can be used in many salads, casseroles and chilli dishes. They are also very tasty with rice. This bean is native to the Americas.

9. Lentils – are available in a variety of sizes and colors, with red, green and brown most common in the West. They all cook very easily and do not need to be soaked beforehand. Some people believe that they are more easily digestible if soaked for a while. Lentils are very high in protein and have a high carbohydrate content— excellent for soups, rissoles, spreads and loaves.

10. Mung Beans – are small olive green beans, originating in Southeast Asia. They contain an exceptionally high proportion of vitamin A, plus vitamins B and C. This is the main bean used for bean sprouts. If cooked, they need to be soaked overnight, drained, rinsed and then cooked for 30 minutes.

11. Peanuts – are a legume and not a nut. They are known in their salted or roasted form, but are grown mainly as a source of vegetable oil. Peanuts contain a high proportion of fatty acids.

12. Pinto Beans – are speckled brown beans from Mexico, also known as refried beans. They can be used in chilli dishes instead of kidney beans.

13. Soya Beans – are the most nutritious of all pulses. They need a long time to cook and very careful flavouring. Tofu is made from soya beans. They contain a high quality protein and also unsaturated fats that can reduce cholesterol levels in the blood. They are the first bean of which written records are available and were recognised by the Chinese at least 2,000 years ago as being one of the main, principal and sacred crops. The others were wheat, barley, rice and millet.

14. Split Peas – are bright green or yellow in colour. They do not need to be soaked overnight. They make excellent soups and purée.

PREPARATION FOR COOKING PULSES

A. With chick peas and lentils, check for little pieces of grit or small stones before washing thoroughly.

B. Red lentils, split peas and black-eyed beans do not need to be soaked overnight.

C. All other beans and pulses need to be rinsed well and soaked overnight. Rinse again and cook 1 part of beans or lentils with 2 parts of water, according to the times mentioned.

D. Put salt with beans after they are soaked, otherwise the outsides become tough and the beans don't cook properly.

SPROUTED BEANS, GRAINS AND LENTILS

Sprouted beans, grains and lentils are very nutritious, rich in vitamins and minerals and contain high-quality protein. They are also very easy to grow. All you need is a wide-necked jar and a piece of cloth secured over the top with an elastic band.

Most grains, seeds and pulses are suitable, the most common being alfalfa seeds, sunflower seeds, adzuki beans, mung beans, chick peas and all kinds of lentils.

A HOTPOT OF TIPS

VEGETABLES

Vegetables should be cooked either conservatively, i.e. in very little water using a tight-lidded pan (heavy-based pans are best) or as a vegetable stew or soup.

Never throw vegetable water away as it contains valuable minerals and vitamins lost from the vegetables. Vegetables should be fresh and cooked for 10-20 minutes according to variety and size. Never overcook as this destroys the vitamin C.

CHEESE

Most hard cheeses are set with rennet derived from an animal source and are therefore unsuitable for vegetarians. This can also apply to soft cheeses, so always check the label. Most supermarkets and health food shops offer a good choice of vegetarian or kosher cheeses nowadays. Kosher cheeses do not contain animal rennet.

JELLYING AGENTS

Gelatine and aspic are derived from the bones or flesh of animals or fish. Vegetable jellying agents are used instead, such as carrageen and agar, which are both from seaweed.

SPICES AND SEASONING

To make your own 'Garam Masala' for Indian dishes, grind together:

1 part cloves
2 parts cinnamon
1 part coriander seeds
1 part ginger
1 part nutmeg
1 part black pepper
2 parts cumin seeds

As referred to earlier, none of the recipes in this cookbook contains onion or garlic. Instead, for added flavor, a pinch of asafoetida (otherwise known as hing) may be used. As a cleansing or disinfecting agent, (e.g. to help deal with colds, catarrh, influenza and so on) use ginger, cinnamon, mustard and mustard seeds.

Thyme, marjoram and other herbs and spices also prevent and allay catarrh, chest troubles, etc.

REPLACEMENT FOR EGGS

The recipes in this book are lacto-vegetarian and therefore do not contain eggs. However, if you want to convert your own favorite recipes, which would normally require up to three eggs, the following can be used as a replacement. For the equivalent of one egg, beat together 1 tablespoon of cornflour, 1 tablespoon of yoghurt and 1 tablespoon of milk. Alternatively, soak dried apricots overnight in water and then blend and strain them, using a spoonful or more of the resulting mixture as required. Commercially produced egg replacement products are also widely available and, as a final option, a cake may often be made by simply omitting any egg content, without substitution.

And a little history with which to end. . . .

The history of vegetarianism is longer than many people might think. In fact, vegetarianism has been a part of cultures all over the world going back thousands of years. One of the early prominent vegetarians was Pythagoras, the 6th Century BC Greek philosopher and mathematician, whose community saw vegetarianism as a contribution to peace. In first century Palestine, the Essenes, a religious group of which Jesus is believed to have been a member, followed a vegetarian diet, as did many

early Christians and church fathers, in a non-violent tradition later exemplified by St. Francis of Assisi. Buddhism, Zoroastrianism and Jainism, amongst other religions and beliefs, have all lent their support to vegetarianism, as well as certain groups in early Egypt. Moving to more modern times, the 18th Century Enlightenment saw a fresh appraisal of humanity's place in the order of things. Many raised moral objections to the mistreatment of animals, while the Romantic poet Shelley also pointed out that a vegetarian diet allowed for a much more efficient use of resources. A cookery book dedicated to vegetarian recipes was published in England as long ago as 1812 and a vegetarian hospital was established in 1846.

ABBREVIATIONS

Throughout this book, both metric and imperial measurements are given. The following terms are used.

C	Centigrade
F	Fahrenheit
tsp	teaspoon
tbs	tablespoon
g	gram
kg	kilogram
ml	milliliter
l	liter
cm	centimeter
oz	ounce
lb	pound
fl oz	fluid ounce
pint	pint
in	inch

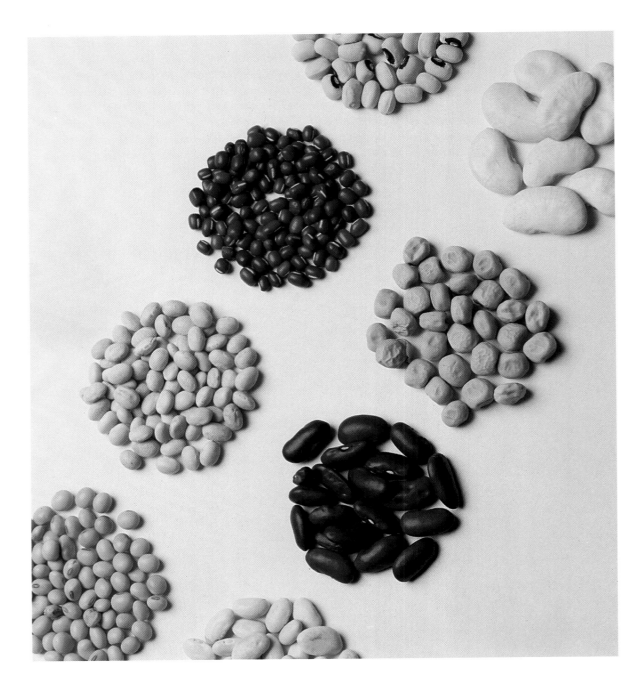

EQUIVALENCE TABLE

WEIGHTS

30	g	(1 oz)
60	g	(2 oz)
90	g	(3 oz)
125	g	(4 oz)
155	g	(5 oz)
185	g	(6 oz)
220	g	(7 oz)
250	g	(8 oz)
280	g	(9 oz)
315	g	(10 oz)
345	g	(11 oz)
375	g	(12 oz)
410	g	(13 oz)
440	g	(14 oz)
470	g	(15 oz)
500	g	(1 lb)
530	g	(17 oz)
560	g	(18 oz)
590	g	(19 oz)
625	g	(1¼ lb)
750	g	(1½ lb)
875	g	(1¾ lb)
1	kg	(2 lb)
1.5	kg	(3 lb)

LIQUID MEASURES

30	ml	(1 fl oz)
60	ml	(2 fl oz)
100	ml	(3 fl oz)
125	ml	(4 fl oz)
150	ml	(¼ pint)
180	ml	(6 fl oz)
210	ml	(7 fl oz)
250	ml	(8 fl oz)
275	ml	(9 fl oz)
300	ml	(½ pint)
330	ml	(11 fl oz)
360	ml	(12 fl oz)
390	ml	(13 fl oz)
420	ml	(14 fl oz)
450	ml	(¾ pint)
500	ml	(16 fl oz)
600	ml	(1 pint)
750	ml	(1¼ pints)
900	ml	(1½ pints)
1.2	l	(2 pints)
1.8	l	(3 pints)

LENGTH

5	mm	(¼ in)
1	cm	(½ in)
2	cm	(¾ in)
2.5	cm	(1 in)
5	cm	(2 in)
8	cm	(3 in)
10	cm	(4 in)
12	cm	(5 in)
15	cm	(6 in)
18	cm	(7 in)
20	cm	(8 in)
23	cm	(9 in)
25	cm	(10 in)
28	cm	(11 in)

OVEN TEMPERATURES

120°C / 250°F / Gas Mark ½

140°C / 275°F / Gas Mark 1

150°C / 300°F / Gas Mark 2

160°C / 325°F / Gas Mark 3

180°C / 350°F / Gas Mark 4

190°C / 375°F / Gas Mark 5

200°C / 400°F / Gas Mark 6

220°C / 425°F / Gas Mark 7

Starters

Avocado and Tomato Spread
Cottage Cheese with Tomato
   Spread
Hummus
Cold Stuffed Peppers
Cheese Paste
Mozzarella Salad
Mushroom and Walnut Paté
Plain Pancakes
Spinach and Potato Patties
Sweetcorn Fritters
Vegetable Pakoras
Walnut Balls
Variety Vegetable Fritters
Sweet and Sour Vegetables
Samosas
Banana and Nut Spread

Avocado and Tomato Spread (Opposite below)

Mash ingredients together and beat until smooth. Keep in an airtight container.

Serve with toast.

1 avocado, peeled
1 large tomato, peeled
a little lemon juice
salt and pepper

Cottage Cheese with Tomato Spread

Cut the tomatoes into small cubes. Put a little butter or margarine into a frying pan and add the ground cumin seeds. Allow the cumin to brown for a couple of seconds, then add tomatoes and a little salt and pepper. Remove from the heat, add cottage cheese and mix. Return to a low flame to warm slightly.

Variation: replace tomatoes with chopped mushrooms.

Serve with rice or on toast.

220 g (7 oz) tomatoes, diced
1 tsp butter OR margarine
pinch of cumin seeds, ground
salt and pepper, to taste
375 g (12 oz) Cottage Cheese (page 212)

Hummus (Opposite above)

Soak the chick peas overnight. Wash and cook in boiling water for 1 hour or until soft. Drain and reserve the water. Place all the ingredients in a blender, add the reserved chick pea water a little at a time and blend to a soft paste. Keep in an airtight container.

500 g (1 lb) white chick peas
2 tbs lemon juice
4 tbs tahini
pinch of asafoetida (hing)
3 tbs olive oil
salt and pepper, to taste

Cold Stuffed Peppers

Cut the tops off the peppers, save the tops and discard the seeds. Mix all the other ingredients together and fill the peppers. Replace the tops. Cover with cling film and leave in the refrigerator to set for 1-2 hours.

Serve with salad.

SERVES 3.

4 green peppers
440 g (14 oz) cream cheese
125 g (4 oz) Cheddar OR Muenster cheese, grated
60 ml (2 fl oz) buttermilk
1 small potato, boiled, peeled and diced

Cheese Paste

Mix all the ingredients to form a paste. For a softer mixture, add extra milk.

Serve with toast.

250 g (8 oz) Cheddar cheese, grated
60 g (2 oz) butter OR margarine
½ tsp salt
¼ tsp black pepper
¼ tsp mustard
3-5 tbs milk
30 g (1 oz) olives, finely chopped (optional)

Mozzarella Salad (Opposite)

Thinly slice the Mozzarella balls. Slice the tomatoes horizontally to make rings. Arrange Mozzarella and tomato rings alternately on a large plate. Pour oil over sparingly and sprinkle with chopped basil. Add salt and pepper to taste. Lemon juice can also be squeezed over.

Serve with breads such as Focaccia (page 181).

SERVES 4.

2 Mozzarella balls
4 tomatoes
2 tbs olive oil
fresh basil, whole OR chopped
salt and pepper
lemon juice (optional)

Mushroom and Walnut Paté

Fry the chopped mushrooms in olive oil, over a low heat, until tender. Mix the walnuts and mushrooms together and add soya sauce, a little at a time, until the consistency is like paté. Add black pepper to taste.

Serve with salad, toast or savoury biscuits.

125 g (4 oz) mushrooms, finely chopped
1 tbs olive oil
125 g (4 oz) walnuts, finely chopped
soya sauce, to mix
black pepper, to taste

Plain Pancakes

Combine the flour, water or milk, salt and pepper and use an electric mixer to make a smooth batter. Heat ½ teaspoon of oil in frying pan and spread the pancake batter evenly in the pan with a spoon. Fry each side until golden brown.

250 g (8 oz) self-raising flour
water OR milk, to mix
salt and pepper, to taste
oil, for frying

Various fillings can be made and rolled into the pancake:
1. **Fried mushrooms seasoned with herbs, salt and pepper.**
2. **Ricotta cheese or Cottage Cheese (page 212).**
3. **Maple syrup.**
4. **Lemon and sugar.**
5. **Chutney or any Pickle (page 90-91).**
6. **Fruit jam (page 202-211).**

MAKES 6 PANCAKES.

Spinach and Potato Patties

Heat 1 tablespoon of oil in a pan and fry the celery gently until softened. Chop the spinach, boil it in a little water and drain it. Thoroughly mix together all the ingredients except the flour and oil. Shape the mixture into 8 large or 16 small balls and flatten them slightly. Coat the balls with flour and fry in hot shallow oil for 2 minutes on each side or until golden brown.

MAKES 8 OR 16 PATTIES.

1 tbs oil
2 sticks celery, finely chopped
1 kg (2 lb) fresh spinach OR
   250 g (8 oz) frozen spinach
500 g (1 lb) potatoes, boiled and mashed
¼ tsp nutmeg
140 g (4½ oz) Cheddar cheese OR
   Cottage Cheese (page 212)
salt and pepper, to taste
flour, for coating
oil, for frying

Sweetcorn Fritters

Put the corn in a bowl. Sift the flour into the bowl and add the salt, pepper and sugar. Then stir in the cream and mix thoroughly. Lightly grease a griddle or large frying pan with oil and heat for a few seconds. Drop spoonfuls of corn batter onto the griddle or pan. Flatten them with a palette knife. Cook for 1-2 minutes until bubbles appear and begin to burst, and the underside is golden brown. Turn the fritter over with a palette knife and cook the other side for 1-2 minutes or until golden brown. Repeat with the remaining batter, keeping the fritters warm until ready to serve.

SERVES 4.

500 g (1 lb) frozen corn
4 tbs self-raising flour
½ tsp salt
½ tsp black pepper, ground
½ tsp caster sugar
150 ml (¼ pint) double cream
oil, for frying

Vegetable Pakoras (Opposite)

Place all the ingredients for the batter in a bowl, except the water and oil. Slowly add in the water until a thick smooth batter is formed. Allow it to stand for about 10 minutes.

Wash and dry the vegetables. Drain them on a paper towel. Do not mix the vegetables as the cooking times vary.

Heat the oil for frying. Dip a few vegetables at a time in the batter until fully coated. Deep fry over a medium heat until golden brown. Drain on a paper towel.

Serve hot with Chutney for Pakoras (page 90).

MAKES 20-25.

BATTER
250 g (8 oz) gram flour (chick pea flour)
90 g (3 oz) coarse semolina
¼ tsp cayenne pepper
salt, to taste
1 tbs fresh ginger, crushed
1 tsp black pepper, crushed
1 tbs lemon juice
handful of fresh coriander, chopped
1 tbs hot oil
1 small pinch of Eno's
180 ml (6 fl oz) water
oil, for deep frying

VEGETABLES
1 aubergine, cut into thin round slices
1 potato, cut into thin round slices
½ medium cauliflower, broken into small florets
1 green pepper, cut round or in thick strips
baby spinach leaves
mushrooms
bananas

Walnut Balls

Blend together the yoghurt, cornflour and milk, then mix all the ingredients together. If the mixture is a little dry, add extra milk. Form the mixture into balls and arrange on a well-greased baking tray. Bake at 180°C/350°F/Gas Mark 4 for 25 minutes or until brown.

MAKES 8-10 BALLS.

1 tbs yoghurt
1 tbs cornflour
1 tbs milk
155 g (5 oz) walnuts, ground
60 g (2 oz) breadcrumbs
125 g (4 oz) mild Cheddar OR Muenster cheese, grated
2 large sticks celery, finely chopped
salt and pepper, to taste
2 tbs parsley
1 large red pepper, finely chopped

Variety Vegetable Fritters (Opposite)

Mix the flour, semolina and water to make a smooth batter. Add the salt, pepper, sugar and fennel seeds and mix. Dip the vegetables of your choice into the batter and deep fry in hot oil until golden brown and tender.

Suitable vegetables are broccoli broken in small florets, cauliflower broken in small florets, button mushrooms, bananas cut in rounds, potatoes cut into thin rounds, aubergines cut into rounds or cubed, chopped spinach, chopped fenugreek, shredded cabbage or spinach, fenugreek and cabbage mixed.

SERVES 20.

125 g (4 oz) gram flour (chick pea flour)
60 g (2 oz) semolina
water, to mix
salt and pepper, to taste
1 tsp sugar
1 tbs fennel seeds
500 g (1 lb) vegetables
oil, for deep frying

Sweet and Sour Vegetables (Opposite)

Prepare all the vegetables separately. Heat 1 tablespoon of oil in a wok, add ginger and fry for ½ a minute. Add a little oil and vegetables, one at a time, and cook on a high heat, tossing and turning until crisp. Add 1 tablespoon of soya sauce whilst stir-frying. Fry each type of vegetable separately using this method. Deep fry the tofu. Reserve the juice from the pineapple or lychees. Transfer all the stir-fried vegetables, tofu and pineapple or lychees to a large serving bowl and toss gently. Heat a little oil in a pan and fry the ginger until slightly brown. Add the juice from the pineapple or lychees, tomato purée, tomatoes, vinegar, water and sugar. Mix the water and cornflour together, and when the consistency is creamy, pour it slowly into the tomato sauce, stirring all the time. Cook until the sauce thickens. Taste for sweetness and sourness. Add more sugar or vinegar accordingly. Simmer for a further 10 minutes, then pour over the vegetables.

Optional: blanch walnuts in boiling water. Make a batter by using 125 g (4 oz) rice flour, 125 ml (4 fl oz) water, pinch of baking powder, salt and pepper. Dip blanched walnuts into the batter and deep fry until golden brown. Mix with vegetables.

Serve with rice or rice noodles.

SERVES 6-8.

6 tbs oil
60 g (2 oz) ginger root, finely grated
2 green peppers, chopped
250 g (8 oz) mushrooms, chopped
250 g (8 oz) carrots, sliced round
4 tbs soya sauce
250 g (8 oz) hard tofu, cubed
oil, for deep frying
375 g (12 oz) canned pineapple chunks OR lychees
125 g (4 oz) walnuts (optional)

SAUCE
1 tbs oil
1 tsp ginger root, crushed
juice from canned pineapple OR lychees
2 tbs tomato purée
470 g (15 oz) canned tomatoes, liquidised
2 tbs vinegar, cider or balsamic
water, to mix
3 tbs granulated sugar
300 ml (½ pint) water
3 tbs cornflour

Samosas (Opposite)

Mix flour, salt, lemon juice and oil in a bowl, with enough cold water to make a soft manageable dough. Cover and leave to one side.

Heat 2-3 tablespoons of oil in a saucepan and put in the cumin seeds. When the cumin seeds are brown, add the vegetables. Stir, cover and allow the vegetables to cook for 10-15 minutes over a low heat, making sure the vegetables don't mash. Add in lemon juice, garam masala, salt and pepper and cook for a further 2-3 minutes. Put the vegetable mixture in a big tray to cool quickly.

Divide the dough into small balls, the size of a walnut. Roll each ball out into rounds of 8-10 cm (3-4 in) in diameter, and cut them in half. Place the filling on one half of each semi-circle. Moisten the edge of the pastry with a little water, fold over the other side and seal by pressing and twisting over slightly.

Samosas must be well sealed so that they don't come apart whilst frying. Heat the oil in a frying pan and deep fry the samosas until golden brown.

Serve with Chutney (page 90-91).

MAKES 10-12 SAMOSAS.

PASTRY
250 g (8 oz) plain flour
1 tsp salt
1 tbs lemon juice
1 tbs oil

FILLING
2-3 tbs oil
1 tbs cumin seeds
1-2 medium size potatoes, diced small
1 carrot, diced small
1-2 tbs lemon juice
1½ tsp garam masala
1½ tsp salt and pepper, to taste
oil, for deep frying

Banana and Nut Spread

Mash avocado and banana. Mix all the ingredients together. Keep in an airtight container.

Serve with toast.

1 avocado, peeled
½ banana, peeled
1 tbs lemon juice
2 tbs walnuts, chopped
2 tbs desiccated coconut

Soups

Aubergine Soup
Bean and Carrot Soup
Lentil and Pumpkin Soup
Broad Bean Soup
Carrot Soup
Broccoli Soup
Celery Soup
Vegetable Soup
Miso Soup
Minestrone Soup
Mushroom Soup
Potato and Celery Soup
Pumpkin Soup
Spinach and Split Pea Soup
Vegetable and Bean Soup
Tomato Soup
Sweetcorn Soup
Vegetable and Barley Soup

Aubergine Soup

Fry the cabbage in oil, with asafoetida, until soft and brown. Add tomatoes and stock and bring to the boil. Add the aubergines and cook until just tender. Add the coconut cream, season to taste and heat through without boiling. Garnish with fresh herbs.

SERVES 6-8.

250 g (8 oz) cabbage, finely shredded
4 tbs oil
1 tsp asafoetida (hing)
4 large tomatoes, chopped
1.8 l (3 pints) stock OR water
4 medium aubergines (eggplant), chopped
150 ml (¼ pint) coconut cream
salt and pepper, to taste
handful of fresh herbs, finely chopped

Bean and Carrot Soup

Drain and rinse the beans, then simmer them for 30 minutes in a large saucepan of boiling water. Add celery, carrots, chopped parsley or basil, and nutmeg. Cook together for another 30 minutes until the beans are tender. Add a knob of butter for garnish and season to taste.

SERVES 8-10.

125 g (4 oz) haricot beans, soaked overnight
1.2 l (2 pints) boiling water
1 stick celery, sliced
2 large carrots, peeled and diced
30 g (1 oz) fresh parsley OR basil, chopped
pinch of nutmeg
knob (1 tsp) of butter
salt and pepper, to taste

Lentil and Pumpkin Soup (Opposite)

Lightly sauté the pumpkin in vegetable oil for 5 minutes. Add lentils and water and bring to the boil. Simmer for 20-30 minutes and blend. Season with salt and pepper and knob of butter.

SERVES 6-8.

250 g (8 oz) pumpkin, diced
2 tbs vegetable oil
125 g (4 oz) red lentils
1.5 l (2½ pints) water
knob (1 tsp) of butter
salt and pepper, to taste

Broad Bean Soup

Sauté the cabbage in oil, with asafoetida, until brown and soft. Add the broad beans, lemon rind, lemon juice and half of the parsley. Bring to the boil, cover and simmer until the beans are tender. Purée in a blender. Reheat and serve, garnished with the remaining parsley. Season to taste.

SERVES 6-8.

125 g (4 oz) cabbage, shredded
3 tbs cooking oil
pinch of asafoetida (hing)
2.4 l (4 pints) water
500 g (1 lb) broad beans, shelled or frozen
grated rind and juice of 3 lemons
60 g (2 oz) fresh parsley, finely chopped
salt and pepper, to taste

Carrot Soup

Boil the carrots in water until just tender. Allow to cool. Blend the carrots and water in a blender. Return blended carrots to the saucepan, add salt, pepper, ginger and butter and bring back to the boil.

Note: The amount of water can be increased for more sauce or reduced as required. You can even mash a few pieces of potato to thicken the sauce.

SERVES 4.

500 g (1 lb) carrots, peeled and chopped
600 ml (1 pint) boiling water
salt and pepper, to taste
1 tbs fresh ginger, crushed or grated
knob (1 tsp) of butter
1 potato

Broccoli Soup

Simmer the broccoli and potatoes in milk and water for 15-20 minutes. Remove the vegetables and some of the liquid, and blend well. Return the blended mixture to the rest of the liquid. Add more water if necessary. Add the seasoning and a knob of butter and mix well.

Serve with hot buttered toast or croutons.

SERVES 8.

1 kg (2 lb) broccoli, finely chopped
3 potatoes, cubed
300 ml (½ pint) milk
600 ml (1 pint) water
salt and pepper, to taste
knob (1 tsp) of butter

Celery Soup

Boil the celery in water for 10-15 minutes. Allow to cool, then blend for a couple of minutes. Return blended celery to saucepan and bring back to the boil, adding milk, cornflour, butter, salt and pepper. Continue to stir until it thickens.

Serve hot.

SERVES 5-6.

4-6 sticks celery, quartered
600 ml (1 pint) boiling water
150 ml (¼ pint) milk
1 tbs cornflour
knob (1 tsp) of butter
salt and pepper, to taste

Vegetable Soup

Boil all the vegetables until soft, keeping the water. Blend the vegetables until puréed. Sieve into another saucepan, adding the water from the vegetables. Add more water for a thinner soup. Bring back to the boil, adding the butter. Garnish with parsley and season with salt and pepper.

SERVES 4-6.

1-2 potatoes, peeled and chopped
125 g (4 oz) cabbage, chopped
1-2 carrots, chopped
1-2 tomatoes
90 g (3 oz) peas
900 ml (1½ pints) boiling water
knob (1 tsp) of butter
handful of fresh parsley
salt and pepper to taste

Miso Soup

Bring the water to the boil, add vegetables and simmer for 15 minutes. Dilute miso in a little water and add to the soup with the grated ginger. Turn off the heat and leave for 5 minutes with the lid on.

SERVES 4-6.

900 ml (1½ pints) water
2 carrots, thinly sliced
1 small turnip, thinly sliced
2–3 cabbage leaves, thinly shredded
1 tbs of miso (made from soya beans)
1½ tbs fresh ginger, grated

Minestrone Soup (Opposite)

Sauté all the vegetables in oil in a fairly large pan until they are golden. Add enough water or vegetable stock to cover the vegetables and beans. Add mixed herbs, tomato purée and soya chunks. Simmer until all the vegetables are cooked. Season to taste and serve.

SERVES 6-8.

2 carrots, diced
250 g (8 oz) broccoli, broken into small florets
125 g (4 oz) cauliflower, broken into small florets
2 potatoes, diced
1 small turnip
60 g (2 oz) canned red kidney beans
60 g (2 oz) French beans
3 tbs oil
600 ml (1 pint) boiling water OR vegetable stock
1 tbs mixed herbs
2 tbs tomato purée
125 g (4 oz) soya chunks
salt and pepper, to taste

Mushroom Soup

Put the water into a saucepan with butter or margarine and mushrooms. Cook until soft and tender. Add salt, pepper, cornflour and herbs. When mixed, slowly add milk, stirring continuously until the soup is thick and creamy.

SERVES 4-6.

300 ml (½ pint) water
1 tbs butter OR margarine
500 g (1 lb) fresh mushrooms, sliced
salt and pepper, to taste
2 tbs cornflour
1 tsp herbs
300 ml (½ pint) milk

Potato and Celery Soup

Sauté celery in oil in a saucepan and season with salt and pepper. Add water and potatoes. Bring to the boil and simmer until the potatoes are soft. Add the butter and whisk the soup until it is creamy.
Add a little milk or single cream for richness.

SERVES 4-6.

4 sticks celery, finely chopped
2 tbs oil
salt and pepper, to taste
900 ml (1½ pints) water
5 small potatoes, peeled and cubed
knob (1 tsp) of butter
milk OR single cream (optional)

Pumpkin Soup

Put vegetables in a saucepan with cold water. Bring to the boil and simmer for 20 minutes. Blend into a thick purée. Add salt and pepper. Garnish with parsley and butter.

In winter add grated ginger.

SERVES 6-8.

1 small pumpkin, peeled and cubed
1 small potato
1.2 l (2 pints) water
salt and pepper, to taste
1 tbs parsley
knob (1 tsp) of butter

Spinach and Split Pea Soup

Heat the oil in a saucepan, add the spinach and cook for 5 minutes. Wash the split peas. Add peas and water to the spinach and simmer until the peas are cooked. Add salt, pepper, ginger and tomato purée.

Serve with rice.

SERVES 4-6.

2 tbs oil
500 g (1 lb) spinach, washed and chopped
125 g (4 oz) yellow split peas
900 ml (1½ pints) cold water
salt and pepper, to taste
1 tbs fresh ginger, crushed or grated
½ tbs tomato purée (optional)

Vegetable and Bean Soup

Top and tail the runner beans and cut into short lengths. Put the water or stock in a large saucepan with the oil and add all the vegetables. Cover and cook over a medium heat for 30 minutes until the vegetables are tender. Add the macaroni and cook for a further 10 minutes. Serve the soup in individual bowls and, just before serving, garnish with parsley, salt and pepper and sprinkle with cheese.

SERVES 8-10.

125 g (4 oz) runner beans
155 g (5 oz) kidney beans, soaked overnight
1.5 l (2½ pints) boiling water OR vegetable stock
3 tbs olive oil
1 large carrot, diced
½ small cauliflower, broken into small florets
2 stalks celery, chopped
2 medium potatoes, peeled and diced
60 g (2 oz) small whole-wheat macaroni
handful of fresh parsley, finely chopped
cheese, to garnish
salt and pepper, to taste

23

Tomato Soup (Opposite)

Blend the tomatoes with water. Sieve the mixture through a large strainer into a saucepan and add tomato purée, blended potato, sugar, salt and pepper. Bring to the boil and simmer for about 20 minutes, then add the knob of butter. Remove from the heat. Add the cream just before serving and garnish with parsley.

SERVES 4-6.

500 g (1 lb) tomatoes
600 ml (1 pint) water
1 tbs tomato purée
1 large potato, boiled and mashed
1 tsp sugar
salt and pepper, to taste
knob (1 tsp) of butter
300 ml (½ pint) double cream
1 tbs fresh parsley, chopped

Sweetcorn Soup

Boil the corn in water for 5-10 minutes. Blend until it becomes creamy. Return blended corn to the saucepan and simmer gently for 10-15 minutes. Add salt, pepper and butter. Garnish with parsley.

SERVES 4.

500 g (1 lb) frozen corn
900 ml (1½ pints) boiling water
salt and pepper, to taste
knob (1 tsp) of butter
2 tbs fresh parsley, chopped

Vegetable and Barley Soup

Drain and rinse the barley. Place it in a pan, cover with water and boil for 30-40 minutes until cooked.

Heat the oil in large saucepan, add the cabbage and stir over a medium heat until brown. Add carrots, potatoes, celery, tomatoes, salt, pepper and the cooked barley with its water. Bring to the boil. Reduce heat, cover and simmer for about 15 minutes until the vegetables are tender. Garnish with parsley before serving.

SERVES 4-6.

60 g (2 oz) pearl barley, soaked overnight
900 ml (1½ pints) boiling water
1 tbs oil
90 g (3 oz) cabbage, shredded
2 carrots, chopped
1 potato, chopped
1 stick celery, chopped
400 g (14 oz) canned tomatoes
salt and pepper, to taste
2 tbs fresh parsley, chopped

Salads
and
Dressings

Avocado Salad

Peel the avocados and cut into small pieces. Place in a bowl with sliced mushrooms. Pour Herb Dressing over the salad and mix together.

Serve with wholemeal bread and butter or toast.

SERVES 4.

2 avocados
140 g (4½ oz) mushrooms, sliced
4 tbs Herb Dressing (page 40)

Baby Potato Salad

Boil the potatoes in their skins until just tender. Rub off the skins and cut into quarters. Pour Vinaigrette Sauce on top, and sprinkle with fresh chopped mint.

SERVES 4-5.

500 g (1 lb) small new potatoes
3-4 tbs Vinaigrette Sauce (page 43)
handful of fresh mint

Couscous Salad (Opposite)

Boil the water. Put the couscous in a bowl and pour the water over. Set aside to stand for 10 minutes, then drain. Combine couscous with all the salad ingredients and toss together. Pour the salad dressing over the top and toss again. Garnish with basil.

SERVES 6-8.

250 ml (8 fl oz) water
185 g (6 oz) couscous
1 carrot, finely diced
1 red pepper, finely diced
1 tomato, finely diced
1 small cucumber, finely diced
3-4 lettuce leaves, finely chopped
60 ml (2 fl oz) Mustard Dressing OR
  Vinaigrette Sauce (page 43)
handful of fresh basil, chopped

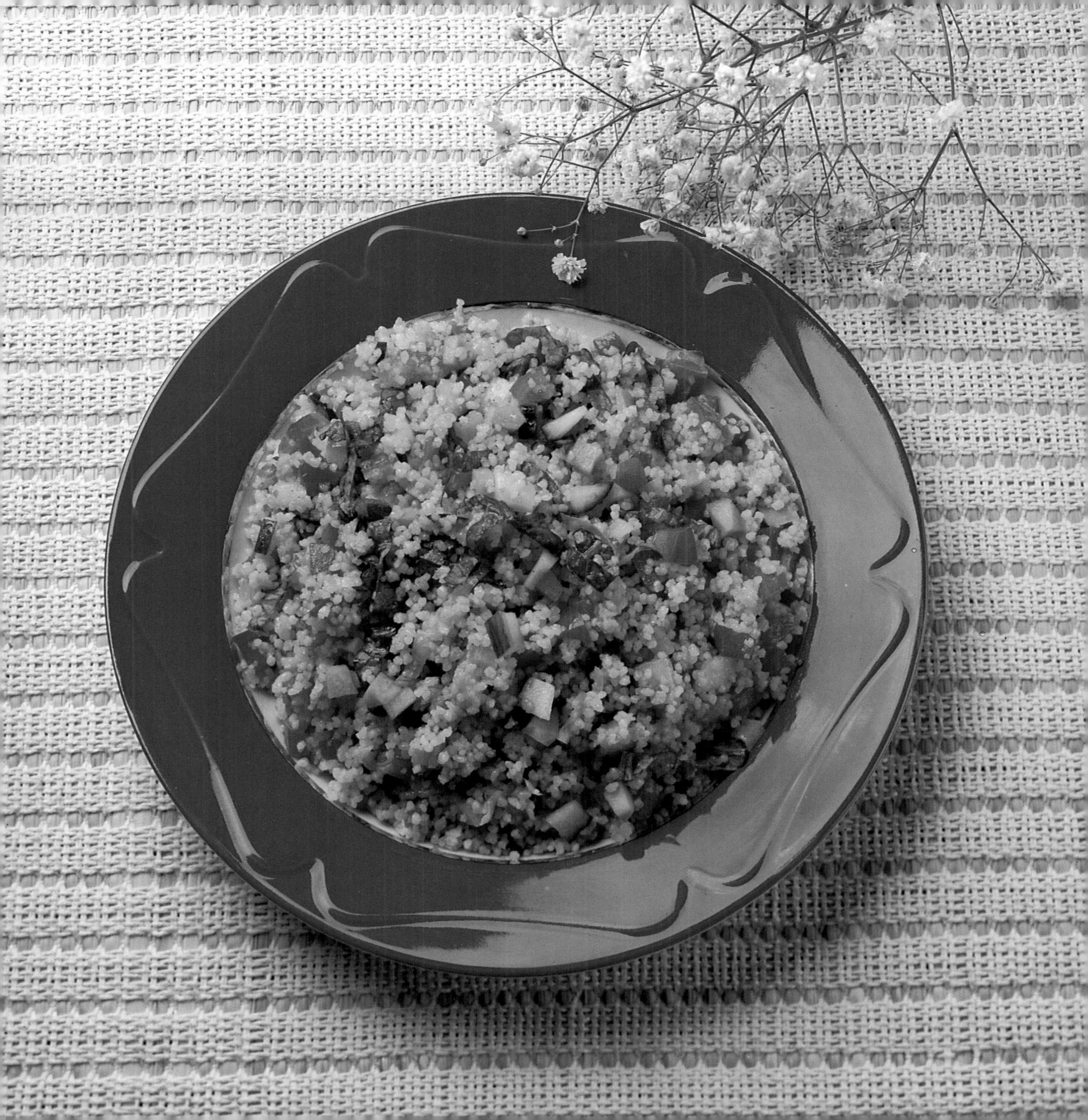

Bean Sprout Salad

Grill the sesame seeds for 2-3 minutes or until golden brown. Combine sesame seeds, bean sprouts and peppers in a large bowl. Pour the olive oil, lemon juice and soya sauce over and toss well. Refrigerate and leave to stand for a while. Toss again before serving.

SERVES 4-6.

60 g (2 oz) sesame seeds
500 g (1 lb) bean sprouts
1 red pepper, sliced
1 green pepper, sliced
2 tbs olive oil
2 tbs lemon juice
2 tbs light soya sauce

Beetroot and Apple Salad

Wash the lettuce leaves, dry well and place on a serving plate. Cut the beetroot into small cubes. Core the apple and cut into small cubes. Arrange beetroot, apple and walnut on top of the lettuce leaves.

Serve with Yoghurt Dressing.

SERVES 3.

4 lettuce leaves
2 small beetroots, cooked and peeled
1 large green apple, skinned
60 g (2 oz) walnuts, coarsely chopped
4 tbs Yoghurt Dressing (page 43)

Broccoli Salad

Steam the broccoli until tender. Leave to cool, then add salt, oil and vinegar and toss lightly.

SERVES 2.

500 g (1 lb) broccoli, broken into florets
½ tsp salt
1 tsp vinegar
1 tsp oil

Butter Bean and Cauliflower Salad

Drain and rinse the butter beans. In a saucepan, cover the beans with cold water. Bring to the boil and boil steadily for 10 minutes. Lower the heat, cover and simmer for 20-25 minutes until tender. Drain and cool. Steam the cauliflower for 3 minutes, drain and cool. Place beans, cauliflower and mushrooms in a bowl. Pour Oregano Dressing over the vegetables and toss lightly.

SERVES 3-4.

140 g (4½ oz) butter beans, soaked overnight
1 small cauliflower, broken into florets
140 g (4½ oz) mushrooms, sliced
6 tbs Oregano Dressing (page 42)

Tomato and Cucumber Salad

Cut cucumber in half lengthways and then into semi-circular slices. Cut tomatoes into segments. Place in a serving bowl. Sprinkle with salt, pepper and oregano. Slowly pour oil on top and mix. Sprinkle with basil and serve.

SERVES 4-5.

½ cucumber, peeled
2 large tomatoes
salt and pepper, to taste
1 tsp oregano
1 tbs olive oil
handful of fresh basil, chopped

Cauliflower and Beetroot Salad

Mix all the ingredients together and chill before serving.

SERVES 4-5.

375 g (12 oz) cauliflower, broken into small florets, lightly cooked
2 beetroots, cooked, peeled and diced
3 tbs Vinaigrette Sauce (page 43)

Cucumber and Grape Salad

Mix all the ingredients together and serve chilled.

SERVES 3-4.

½ cucumber, diced
140 g (4½ oz) green grapes, seedless
150 ml (¼ pint) plain yoghurt
½ tsp honey
1 tsp cumin seeds, ground

Green Salad

Wash the lettuce and dry it well. Wash cucumber and slice thinly. Mix lettuce and cucumber together in a bowl. Pour Olive Oil Dressing over. Serve as a side dish.

SERVES 4.

lettuce
½ cucumber
1 tbs Olive Oil Dressing (page 41)

Cucumber and Walnut Salad

Mix all the ingredients together. Serve chilled.

SERVES 3-4.

½ cucumber, diced
60 g (2 oz) walnuts, chopped
1 tbs lemon juice
2 tbs olive oil
1 tsp dried oregano
salt and pepper

French Bean Salad

Cut the beans in half. Steam until tender. Place on a salad dish, sprinkle with salt, pepper, olive oil and lemon juice and toss. Sprinkle with fresh mint.

SERVES 4-5.

500 g (1 lb) fresh French beans
boiling water, for steaming
salt and pepper, to taste
1 tbs olive oil
1 tbs lemon juice
handful of fresh mint, chopped

Mixed Bean Salad

Drain and rinse the beans. Place them in a saucepan and cover with cold water. Bring to the boil steadily for 20 minutes. Lower the heat, cover and simmer for 20-25 minutes until tender. Drain and cool. Cook the green beans in boiling water for 7–8 minutes and drain. Place all the beans in a bowl and add the dressing whilst still warm. Sprinkle parsley on top.

SERVES 6-8.

140 g (4½ oz) each butter beans, red kidney beans and haricot beans, soaked overnight
140 g (4½ oz) green beans, sliced
4 tbs Oregano Dressing (page 42)
2 tbs parsley, chopped

Mixed Vegetable Salad

When the potatoes are cold, peel and dice them. Add sweetcorn, cucumber and mushrooms. Dice the tomatoes. Dice the pepper after removing seeds.

Blend the oil with the seasonings and vinegar and pour over the salad before serving.

SERVES 4.

375 g (12 oz) baby potatoes, boiled
375 g (12 oz) sweetcorn, frozen
1 small cucumber, diced
125 g (4 oz) button mushrooms, sliced
375 g (12 oz) tomatoes OR 1 red pepper
3 tbs corn oil
pinch of salt, pepper and sugar
1 tbs cider vinegar

Potato Salad (Opposite)

Boil the potatoes until nearly tender. Leave to cool, then peel and cut into chunks. Add Mayonnaise and mix gently. Wash and chop the tomatoes into small cubes, and halve the olives. Mix with the potatoes and serve.

Baby potatoes do not need peeling.

SERVES 4.

500 g (1 lb) potatoes
boiling water, with a pinch of salt
Mayonnaise (page 41)
2-3 fresh tomatoes
60 g (2 oz) olives

Red Cabbage Salad

Mix all the ingredients together with Mayonnaise.

Serve with a salad dressing of your choice (*page 40-43*).

SERVES 4.

250 g (8 oz) red cabbage, finely shredded
1 green apple, cored and finely chopped
2-3 carrots, grated
1 tbs walnuts, chopped
½ quantity of Mayonnaise (page 41)

Rice and Hazelnut Salad

Wash the rice and put in a saucepan with slightly salted cold water. Bring to the boil, then cover, reduce the heat and simmer for 30-40 minutes until tender. Rinse in cold water and drain well. Place in a bowl with the remaining ingredients and toss thoroughly. Transfer to a shallow dish to serve.

SERVES 6-8.

220 g (7 oz) brown rice
450 ml (¾ pint) cold water, slightly salted
75 g (2½ oz) hazelnuts, chopped and toasted
1 green pepper, thinly diced
3 sticks celery, finely chopped
60 g (2 oz) mushrooms, thinly sliced
6 tbs salad dressing of your choice (page 40-43)
3 tbs fresh parsley, chopped

Pasta Salad (Opposite)

Boil the pasta in a large pan of boiling water until just tender. Drain. Rinse with cold water and drain thoroughly. Mix all the other ingredients and add them to the pasta.

Serve with a salad dressing of your choice (page 40-43).

SERVES 3-4.

375 g (12 oz) pasta twists or shells
boiling water, with a pinch of salt and
  a few drops of oil
30 g (1 oz) olives, coarsely chopped
salt and pepper, to taste
1 carrot, grated
60 g (2 oz) broccoli
1 pepper, thin strips
2-3 fresh tomatoes, finely cubed
3 tbs lemon juice

Pasta with Artichokes Salad

Boil pasta in a large pan of boiling water until just tender. Drain. Rinse with cold water and drain thoroughly. Combine with all the other ingredients in a bowl. Pour the salad dressing over, toss the salad and garnish with parsley or basil.

SERVES 4-5.

500 g (1 lb) pasta
boiling water, with a pinch of salt and
  a few drops of oil
500 g (1 lb) tomatoes, chopped
125 g (4 oz) stoneless black olives
345 g (11 oz) canned artichokes
60 ml (2 fl oz) Olive Oil Dressing (page 41)
handful of fresh parsley OR basil

Tofu Salad

Mix together tofu, nuts, vegetables and apple, and arrange on a bed of lettuce leaves. Mix together olive oil, lemon juice, salt and pepper and sprinkle over the salad.

SERVES 6.

280 g (9 oz) tofu, cubed
1 tbs fried cashew nuts, halved
1 cucumber, cubed
1 green pepper, thinly sliced
1 carrot, thinly sliced
1 apple, thinly sliced
5-6 large lettuce leaves
3 tbs olive oil
3 tbs lemon juice
salt and pepper, to taste

Cucumber Raita

Raitas are dressings based on yoghurt.

Sprinkle the cucumbers with salt and leave for half an hour under a weight (such as a saucer) to squeeze out the excess water. Prepare the dressing by mixing the ingredients in a medium-sized bowl. Add the grated cucumber and mix. Transfer to a serving bowl and sprinkle with ground cumin seeds.

Peeled cucumber is much easier to digest.

SERVES 6.

2 cucumbers, peeled and grated
2 tbs sea salt
1 tsp cumin seeds, ground and roasted

DRESSING
150 ml (¼ pint) yoghurt OR sour cream
1 tbs olive oil
1 tbs lemon juice
salt and pepper, to taste

Herb Dressing

Blend all the ingredients together for 2-3 minutes. Pour over the salad just before serving.

150 ml (¼ pint) yoghurt
125 ml (4 fl oz) olive oil
1 tbs fresh parsley
2 tsp fresh mint
2 tsp fresh dill
juice of ½ lemon
salt and pepper, to taste

Lemon Tahini Dressing

Blend all the ingredients together. Pour over the salad just before serving.

4 tbs tahini
4 tbs corn oil
2 tbs water
2 tbs lemon juice
1 tsp soya sauce

Mayonnaise

Pour soya milk into a blender. Pour the oil in very slowly through the lid and blend until the mixture thickens. Pour the mixture into a bowl, add lemon juice and salt, and slowly fold in. Add more lemon juice if necessary for taste. Can be kept in the refrigerator for 2-3 days.

300 ml (½ pint) soya milk
150 ml (¼ pint) olive oil
2 tsp lemon juice
1 tsp salt

Mustard Dressing

Mix the ingredients together thoroughly. Serve over the salad.

2 tsp mustard
6 tbs olive oil
1 tbs honey
1 tbs dried basil
4 tbs lemon juice
salt and pepper, to taste

Olive Oil Dressing

Blend all the ingredients together thoroughly. Use immediately.

4 tbs olive oil
2 tbs fresh parsley, chopped
2 tbs lemon juice
¼ tsp salt

Oregano Dressing

Blend all the ingredients together. Use immediately over the salad.

1 tbs olive oil
vinegar
1 tsp oregano
salt and pepper, to taste

Tomato Purée Dressing

Blend all the ingredients together.

Serve over a savoury pie.

150 ml (¼ pint) plain yoghurt
1 tsp tomato purée
½ tsp cumin seeds, ground
1 tsp coriander seeds, ground
1 tsp honey

Vegetable Raita

Peel and cut potatoes into small cubes and boil until tender. Chop tomatoes coarsely. Slice the celery finely. Cut chilli in half lengthways, remove seeds and chop very finely. Cut cucumber into small cubes. Mix all the ingredients in a bowl. Chill for 1 hour before serving.

SERVES 4-5.

2 medium potatoes
3 tomatoes
2 sticks celery
1 green chilli
7.5 cm (3 in) piece cucumber, peeled
750 ml (1¼ pints) plain yoghurt
¼ tsp black pepper, ground

Vinaigrette Sauce

Blend all the ingredients in a blender. Pour over the salad just before serving.

250 ml (8 fl oz) olive oil
¼ tsp mustard
juice of ½ lemon
salt and pepper, to taste

Vinaigrette Sauce de Luxe

Blend all the ingredients thoroughly. Pour over the salad a few minutes before serving.

Serve over a green salad.

125 ml (4 fl oz) olive oil
125 ml (4 fl oz) cider vinegar OR lemon juice
125 ml (4 fl oz) water
1 tbs mustard, seasoned
1 tbs soya sauce
1 tsp dried basil

Yoghurt Dressing

Place yoghurt in a bowl. Add sugar and pepper. Coarsely crumble in the cheese. Beat well. Pour over the salad just before serving.

150 ml (¼ pint) plain yoghurt
1 tsp sugar
black pepper, to taste
60 g (2 oz) Cheddar cheese, grated OR Feta cheese

43

Main Dishes

Aubergine Casserole
Broccoli and Mushroom Pie
Baked Aubergines
Bean and Potato Pie
Black-Eyed Bean Casserole
Broad Beans with Pasta
Brown Rice Pie
Cannelloni
Cauliflower Fritters
Celery Flan
Chick Pea and Potato Croquettes
Chick Pea Curry (Channa)
Cauliflower Cheese
Chinese Noodles
Enchilada
Jacket Potatoes
Lasagne
Lentil Loaf
Macaroni Cheese
Mushroom and Sweetcorn Curry
Mushroom and Spinach Pie
Nut Roast
Pasta with Aubergine Sauce
Pasta with Ricotta Cheese
Pasta with Tofu and Vegetables
Peas and Potato Curry
Pasties
Potato and Tomato Bake
Potato Burgers

Potato Curry
Pizza
Potato Pie
Pumpkin Pie
Rice and Vegetable Bake
Rice with French Beans
Savoury Pancakes
Spaghetti Bolognese
Spaghetti Bolognese & Soya
   Mince Bake
Soya Burgers
Spicy Burgers
Spinach Flan
Spinach Pie
Stir-Fried Rice
Stuffed Aubergines
Stuffed Cabbage
Vegetable Rolls
Stir-Fried Vegetables
Vegetable Flans
Stuffed Peppers
Vegetable Pancakes
Tagliatelle with Mushrooms
Vegetable Pie
Tofu Flan
Vegetable Rice
Vegetarian Shepherd's Pie
Walnut Cheese Burgers

Aubergine Casserole

Cut aubergine into 1 cm (½ in) slices. Place in a large bowl, cover with boiling water, add vinegar, stand for 15 minutes and then drain. Pat dry with absorbent paper. Dip the slices in milk, then in flour combined with sesame seeds. Heat half the oil in a large frying pan and add half the aubergine in a single layer. Cook for about 2 minutes until brown on each side. Place in a shallow ovenproof dish. Top with half the mushrooms, courgettes and tomatoes and sprinkle with basil. Combine the breadcrumbs and cheese in a bowl and sprinkle half the mixture over the tomatoes. Repeat the layers, finishing with the breadcrumbs and cheese, and dot with butter or margarine.

Bake in the oven at 190°C/375°F/Gas Mark 5 for 30-40 minutes or until the top is golden.

SERVES 6.

1 large aubergine (eggplant)
1 tbs cider vinegar
2 tbs skimmed milk
60 g (2 oz) wholemeal flour
1 tbs sesame seeds
125 ml (4 fl oz) oil
125 g (4 oz) mushrooms, sliced
2 medium courgettes (zucchini), grated
2 medium tomatoes, sliced
1 tbs basil
125 g (4 oz) breadcrumbs
155 g (5 oz) mild Cheddar cheese
30 g (1 oz) melted butter OR margarine

Broccoli and Mushroom Pie (Opposite)

Mix the flour, salt, oil and water to make a firm dough. Roll the pastry out to 5 mm (¼ in) thick. Place on a greased baking tray.
Steam the broccoli for 2-3 minutes. Fry the mushrooms in oil and add to the cheese sauce. Add salt, pepper, parsley and broccoli, then pour onto the pastry.

Bake at 180°C/350°F/Gas Mark 4 for 30 minutes, or until the pastry is cooked.

SERVES 4-6.

PASTRY
250 g (8 oz) self-raising flour
1 tsp salt
3-4 tbs oil
cold water, to mix

FILLING
500 g (1 lb) broccoli, broken into small florets
250 g (8 oz) mushrooms, chopped
3 tbs oil
1 quantity Cheese Sauce (page 89)
salt and pepper, to taste
handful of fresh parsley, chopped

Baked Aubergines

Slice the aubergines 1 cm (½ in) thick, place in a shallow baking dish and pour the olive oil over them. Cover with foil or a lid and bake at 180°C/350°F/Gas Mark 4 for 30 minutes.

Mix the sauce ingredients and spread evenly over the cooked aubergines. Sprinkle cheese thickly on top of the sauce. Bake for a further 25 minutes, uncovered.

Serve with rice and salad.

SERVES 4.

2 large aubergines
4 tbs olive oil
250 g (8 oz) Mozzarella cheese, grated

SAUCE
155 g (5 oz) canned tomato purée
salt and pepper, to taste
1 tsp oregano
2 tbs soya sauce

Bean and Potato Pie

Drain and rinse the beans. Cook them, covered with water, in a pressure cooker until soft and tender. Blend the tomatoes and purée together in a blender. Heat the oil in a saucepan, fry the celery and add the blended tomato, salt, pepper and vinegar. Add the cooked beans and simmer for 20-25 minutes. Peel the potatoes, cut them into pieces and cover them with boiling water in a saucepan. Boil for 15-20 minutes until tender. Drain and mash, adding a little milk and butter or margarine until smooth and creamy. Place the bean mixture in an ovenproof dish. Spoon the mashed potatoes on top and ridge the surface with a fork. Sprinkle cheese on the top and bake in a hot oven at 200°C/400°F/Gas Mark 6 for 30 minutes until golden brown.

SERVES 6.

470 g (15 oz) haricot beans, soaked overnight
boiling water, to cover
440 g (14 oz) canned tomatoes
2-3 tbs tomato purée
2 tbs oil
4 sticks celery, finely chopped
salt and pepper, to taste
3 tbs vinegar (cider, malt or balsamic)
500 g (1 lb) potatoes
boiling water, with a pinch of salt
250 ml (8 fl oz) milk
4 tbs butter OR margarine
185 g (6 oz) Cheddar cheese, grated

Black-Eyed Bean Casserole

Soak the beans in hot water for at least an hour or soak them overnight. Drain and rinse, then cover with fresh water and boil until tender. Drain and leave aside. Meanwhile heat the oil in a pan, add asafoetida and cabbage and fry until browned. Stir in potatoes, carrots, parsnip and celery. Cover the pan and cook over a low heat for 10 minutes, stirring occasionally to prevent the vegetables from sticking. Stir in cooked beans with water; add herbs, salt and pepper. Pour in water or vegetable stock, adding more if necessary so that all the vegetables are covered. Stir in the tomato purée and treacle and cook on low heat for 1 hour. Sprinkle with grated cheese before serving.

SERVES 4-6.

250 g (8 oz) black-eyed beans
boiling water, to cover
3 tbs oil
pinch of asafoetida (hing)
125 g (4 oz) cabbage, grated
1 large potato, peeled and diced
2 carrots, diced
1 parsnip, peeled and diced
2 sticks celery, chopped
2 tsp mixed herbs
salt and pepper, to taste
600 ml (1 pint) water OR vegetable stock
2 tbs tomato purée
2 tbs treacle
125 g (4 oz) mild Cheddar cheese, grated (optional)

Broad Beans with Pasta

Heat the oil in a pan and cook the broad beans for 10 minutes. Add the mushrooms and tomatoes and cook for a further 10 minutes. Add salt, pepper and parsley. Mix with the pasta, sprinkle with cheese and serve.

SERVES 3.

2 tbs oil
1 kg (2 lb) frozen broad beans
125 g (4 oz) mushrooms, chopped
440 g (14 oz) tomatoes, chopped
salt and pepper, to taste
1 tsp parsley
560 g (18 oz) pasta, cooked and drained
60 g (2 oz) Parmesan cheese, grated

Brown Rice Pie

Combine the ingredients in a bowl and mix thoroughly to make a firm consistency. Grease a baking tray and spread the mixture evenly, pressing with back of a wooden spoon.

Sprinkle extra cheese on top and bake at 200°C/400°F/Gas Mark 6 for 40 minutes or until firm.

SERVES 5-6.

375 g (12 oz) brown rice, cooked
8 tbs Cheddar cheese, grated
2 red peppers
3 carrots, grated
½ Chinese cabbage or white cabbage, finely chopped
250 ml (8 fl oz) plain yoghurt
2 tsp pepper
salt to taste
125 g (4 oz) mixed nuts, chopped
handful of fresh parsley, chopped
125 g (4 oz) gram flour (chick pea flour)
cheese, grated for sprinkling

Cannelloni (Opposite)

Cook the spinach for 5 minutes in 1 teaspoon of oil, strain and put in a bowl. Mix with Ricotta cheese. Heat 2 teaspoon of oil in a pan, add pepper and fry for 2-3 minutes or until tender. Mix with the spinach and Ricotta cheese. Add basil, salt and pepper to the mixture. Fill the cannelloni tubes with the stuffing and place on a greased baking dish.

Chop and liquidise the tomatoes. Heat the oil in a saucepan. Add the tomatoes, basil, salt and pepper and cook until thickened. Pour over the cannelloni. Sprinkle with cheese.

Bake at 200°C/400°F/Gas Mark 6 for 35-40 minutes.

SERVES 6.

STUFFING
1 kg (2 lb) spinach, washed and chopped
3 tbs oil
250 g (8 oz) Ricotta cheese
1 green pepper, chopped
1 tbs fresh basil
salt and pepper, to taste
18 cannelloni, tubes (pre-cooked)

SAUCE
4–5 large tomatoes
3 tbs oil
2 tbs fresh basil, chopped
salt and pepper, to taste
2-3 tbs mild Cheddar cheese, grated

Cauliflower Fritters

Mix flour, water, salt and pepper in a mixing bowl. Beat with an electric mixer to make a fairly thick, smooth batter. Add more water if the batter is too thick. Dip a few florets at a time into the batter and deep fry in hot oil until golden brown.

Serve with cooked rice, vegetables and Sweet and Sour Sauce (page 89).

SERVES 4.

315 g (10 oz) self-raising flour
250 ml (8 fl oz) water
salt and pepper, to taste
1 small cauliflower, broken into florets
oil, for frying

Celery Flan

Put the flour, oatmeal and margarine in a bowl and rub them together until the mixture resembles breadcrumbs. Add water to make a firm dough. Turn onto a floured surface and knead lightly until smooth. Roll out and line a 20 cm (8 in) flan dish. Chill for 15 minutes.

Heat the oil in a pan and gently fry the celery until softened. Beat together the remaining ingredients and pour onto the pastry.

Bake at 190°C/375°F/Gas Mark 5 for 35-40 minutes.

SERVES 4-5.

PASTRY
125 g (4 oz) wholemeal flour
125 g (4 oz) medium oatmeal
125 g (4 oz) margarine
2-3 tbs water

FILLING
2 tbs oil
2 sticks celery, chopped
2 tbs yoghurt
2 tbs cornflour
2 tbs milk
150 ml (5 fl oz) milk
280 g (9 oz) strong Cheddar
*   cheese, grated*
salt and pepper, to taste

Chick Pea and Potato Croquettes

Mix chick peas with potatoes, paprika and parsley. Season with salt and pepper. Form into croquettes. If desired, roll in breadcrumbs or wholemeal flour. Fry in hot shallow oil until crisp and brown, then drain on absorbent paper.

Serve with Tomato Sauce (page 89) and a salad.

MAKES 20 CROQUETTES.

185 g (6 oz) chick peas, soaked, cooked,
  drained and mashed
500 g (1 lb) potatoes, peeled, cooked and mashed
½ tsp paprika
2 tsp fresh parsley, chopped
sea salt, to taste
freshly ground black pepper, to taste
breadcrumbs OR wholemeal flour,
  for coating (optional)
oil, for frying

Chick Pea Curry (Channa)

If using dry chick peas, drain and rinse them. Boil them in a pressure cooker, with enough water to cover, until soft (approximately 30 minutes). If using canned chick peas, drain them, rinse them well and heat them up in a little water.

In a large saucepan, fry the asafoetida and cumin seeds in the oil. Then add the ginger and green chilli. Finally, add the tomatoes, turmeric, chilli powder and garam masala. Continue to cook until the tomatoes have turned into gravy. In the meantime, mash a handful of the chick peas and add to the tomato gravy to thicken the sauce. Add the tamarind water and mix in the remaining chick peas. Simmer for 20 minutes. Add salt to taste.

Serve with Bhatura (page 89) or other bread.

SERVES 4-5.

250 g (8 oz) dry chick peas (channa), soaked
  overnight OR 750 g (1½ lb) canned chick peas
boiling water, to cover
pinch of asafoetida (hing)
2 tsp cumin seeds
2 tbsp oil
30 g (1 oz) fresh ginger, chopped
1 fresh green chilli (optional)
2 large tomatoes, finely chopped
½ tsp turmeric, ground
1 tsp channa masala (can buy it in shops)
½ tsp garam masala (optional)
2 tbs tamarind water (soak a 25 mm [1 in] square
  of tamarind in warm water. When the tamarind
  has softened, squeeze out the water and throw
  away the pulp)
salt, to taste

Cauliflower Cheese (Opposite)

To prepare the cauliflower, remove the outside leaves, break it into large florets and wash and drain them. Cook them in boiling water for 7-10 minutes, then drain. Make the Cheese Sauce according to the recipe. Grease a 25 x 30 cm (10 x 12 in) ovenproof dish. Fill it with the cauliflower and the Cheese Sauce. Sprinkle grated cheese on top.

Bake in the oven at 180°C/350°F/Gas Mark 4 for 20-25 minutes.

SERVES 4.

1 large cauliflower
Cheese Sauce (page 89)
30 g (1 oz) strong Cheddar cheese, grated

Chinese Noodles

Cook noodles in boiling water for 5-8 minutes. Drain and rinse with cold water. Heat oil in a wok or suitable pan and fry the carrots, add peppers and lastly the mushrooms. Add 1-2 tablespoons soya sauce and toss. Cook for 10 minutes. Add cooked noodles, mix well and add 2 more tablespoons of soya sauce.

SERVES 4-6.

500 g (1 lb) Chinese noodles
boiling water, with a pinch of salt
2 tbs cooking oil
125 g (4 oz) carrots, sliced round
125 g (4 oz) green peppers, cut into long strips
125 g (4 oz) mushrooms, chopped
4 tbs soya sauce

Enchilada

Mix together all the sauce ingredients and cook them over a low heat for about 25 minutes.

To make the filling, drain and rinse the beans thoroughly with water and partially mash them. Heat the oil or butter in a pan and stir fry the mushrooms. Add the carrot and green peppers. When half cooked, add the mashed beans. Add enough of the tomato sauce to form into a thick filling.

To make the tortillas, rub the butter or margarine into the flour. Add the salt and bind into a soft dough using the milk and water mixture. Cover and leave for about 10 minutes. Knead well, divide into 12 balls and roll out into slightly thick chapatis. Quickly cook both sides in a frying pan and stack up on a slightly moist cloth.

Thoroughly oil the base of a deep baking tray. Take 1 tortilla, put about a tablespoon of filling mixture in the centre and fold both sides over the mixture. Fill up the remaining tortillas and arrange them in the tray. Spread the sauce over the filled tortillas and sprinkle with cheese.

Bake in the oven at 180°C/350°F/Gas Mark 4 until the cheese has melted. Garnish with chopped parsley.

Serve hot with a crisp salad.

MAKES 12 ENCHILADAS.

SAUCE
750 g (1½ lb) canned peeled tomatoes, liquidised OR creamed tomatoes
pinch of mixed herbs
lemon juice, to taste
green chillies, finely chopped
pinch of sugar
pinch of salt

FILLING
440 g (14 oz) canned red kidney beans
2 tbs oil OR ½ tbs butter OR margarine
125 g (4 oz) mushrooms, sliced
1 medium carrot, diced
2 green peppers, diced

TORTILLAS
375 g (12 oz) self-raising flour
60 g (2 oz) butter
1 tsp salt
150 ml (¼ pint) warm milk and water (½ of each)

TOPPING
250 g (8 oz) mild Cheddar cheese, grated
handful of parsley, chopped

Jacket Potatoes

Scrub the potatoes, prick them with a fork and bake them at 220°C/425°F/Gas Mark 7 until thoroughly cooked. Cut in half and scoop out the flesh. Mash the flesh with salt, pepper and butter or margarine and put back into the jackets. Sprinkle with cheese, place on a tray and bake for 10 more minutes or grill for 2-3 minutes.

SERVES 6.

6 large potatoes
90 g (3 oz) melted butter OR margarine
300 ml (½ pint) double cream
salt and pepper, to taste
90 g (3 oz) Cheddar cheese, finely grated

Lasagne

Set the oven to 190°C/375°F/Gas Mark 5. Chop and liquidise the tomatoes and pour into a bowl. Add salt, pepper, sugar and oil. Spread one large spoonful over the bottom of a 10 cm (4 in) deep ovenproof dish. Place sheets of lasagne over the sauce, until covered. Add layers of mushrooms, soya mince, parsley, cheese, and white sauce. Repeat 3-4 times, alternating layers of tomato sauce, lasagne sheets and the other ingredients. Sprinkle extra cheese on the last layer and bake in the oven for 30 minutes.

SERVES 4.

440 g (14 oz) canned tomatoes
salt and pepper, to taste
1 tsp sugar
4 tbs oil
1 kg (2 lb) pre-cooked lasagne
500 g (1 lb) mushrooms, chopped
250 g (8 oz) soya mince
1 tbs fresh parsley
250 g (8 oz) Mozzarella cheese, grated
600 ml (1 pint) White Sauce (page 89)

Lentil Loaf

Drain and rinse the lentils. Put them into a saucepan, cover with boiling water and simmer until tender. Drain and mash the lentils.

In another saucepan, sauté the asafoetida in a little oil. Mix lentils, asafoetida and all other ingredients in a large bowl. Press into 3 greased loaf tins.

Bake at 180°C/350°F/Gas Mark 4 for 1 hour.

Suggestion: use pecans or walnuts.
Serve with a salad.

MAKES 3 LOAVES.

500 g (1 lb) lentils, soaked overnight
boiling water, to cover
½ tsp asafoetida (hing)
60 ml (2 fl oz) oil
250 g (8 oz) mixed nuts, ground
60 g (2 oz) sunflower seeds
125 g (4 oz) oatmeal
60 g (2 oz) wheatgerm
2-3 sticks celery
½ tsp sage
½ tsp celery seeds, ground
4 tsp soya sauce
salt and pepper, to taste

Macaroni Cheese

Fill a large saucepan ¾ full with water, bring to the boil, then add macaroni and cook until just tender. Meanwhile, prepare the Cheese Sauce. Drain the macaroni, mix with half the Cheese Sauce and place in a deep 25-30 cm (10-12 in) ovenproof dish. Spread the remaining sauce on the top. Sprinkle with parsley and cheese.

Grill until golden-brown or bake in the oven at 200°C/400°F/Gas Mark 6 for 10 minutes.

SERVES 4-5.

500 g (1 lb) macaroni OR any small pasta
boiling water, with a pinch of salt and a
* few drops of oil*
600 ml (1 pint) Cheese Sauce (page 89)
handful of fresh parsley, chopped
125 g (4 oz) strong Cheddar cheese, grated

Mushroom and Sweetcorn Curry

Fry cumin seeds and add curry leaves, green chillies and ground cashew nuts in the oil. Fry until the ground cashew nuts change colour slightly. Add garam masala, liquidised tomato and the tomato purée. After cooking for 5 minutes, add the mushrooms, corn, salt and pepper and simmer for approximately 10-15 minutes. Take the pan off the heat and add fresh cream and coriander.

Serve with rice or Chapatis (page 179).

SERVES 4.

1 tsp cumin seeds
10 curry leaves
2-3 tbs cashew nuts, ground
1-2 tbs oil
1 green chilli, chopped
1 tsp garam masala
300 g (9½ oz) canned tomatoes, liquidised
1 tsp tomato purée
500 g (1 lb) small button mushrooms, halved
440 g (14 oz) canned corn kernels
salt and pepper, to taste
1-2 tbs fresh cream
handful of fresh coriander leaves, chopped

Mushroom and Spinach Pie

Put the flours and butter or margarine into a bowl and rub together lightly until the mixture resembles fine breadcrumbs. Add enough water to make a firm dough. Roll out two-thirds of the pastry thinly and line the bottom and sides of a 28 cm (11 in) flan dish.

Heat half the oil in a saucepan, add the cabbage and fry until softened. Add spinach, nutmeg, salt and pepper and cook gently for 5 minutes. Allow to cool. Fry the mushrooms gently in a separate pan with the rest of the oil. Spread half the spinach mixture on the pastry, place the mushrooms on top and cover with the remaining spinach mixture. Roll out the remaining pastry for a lid for the pie. Cut a slit in the centre of the lid.

Bake at 200°C/400°F/Gas Mark 6 for 30-35 minutes or until the pastry is golden brown.

SERVES 6.

PASTRY
280 g (9 oz) plain flour
140 g (4½ oz) self-raising flour
185 g (6 oz) butter OR margarine
3-4 tbs cold water

FILLING
3 tbs oil
90 g (3 oz) cabbage, finely shredded
500 g (1 lb) spinach, chopped and lightly cooked
pinch of nutmeg, ground
salt and pepper, to taste
250 g (8 oz) mushrooms, sliced
1 tbs sesame seeds

Nut Roast

Fry the cabbage, mushrooms and soya mince separately in oil. Mix all the ingredients together in a bowl to form a soft mixture. Add more milk if needed. Place in 2 greased loaf tins and bake at 180°C/350°F/Gas Mark 4 for 1 hour or until golden brown.

MAKES 2 LOAVES.

60 g (2 oz) cabbage, shredded
125 g (4 oz) mushrooms, sliced
125 g (4 oz) soya mince
4 tbs oil
125 g (4 oz) hazelnuts or walnuts, ground
125 g (4 oz) breadcrumbs
125 g (4 oz) peanuts, ground
1 tsp fresh parsley, chopped
1 tsp mixed herbs
salt and pepper, to taste
60 g (2 oz) strong Cheddar cheese, grated
125 ml (4 fl oz) milk

Pasta with Aubergine Sauce (Opposite)

Fill a large saucepan ¾ full with water, bring to the boil, then add pasta and cook until just tender. Drain well. Wash and dice the vegetables of your choice. Heat 2 tablespoons of oil in a saucepan, add the vegetables and fry until cooked. Add tomatoes and simmer for 5-10 minutes. Add herbs, lemon juice, salt, pepper and chilli. Mix the pasta with the cooked vegetables and cheese.

SERVES 5-6.

500 g (1 lb) pasta
boiling water, with a pinch of salt and
  a few drops of oil
1 aubergine OR other vegetables
2 tbs oil
4-5 tomatoes, chopped
handful of fresh parsley OR 1 tbs dried
  mixed herbs
1 tbs lemon juice
salt and pepper, to taste
1 green chilli (optional)
125 g (4 oz) Parmesan cheese, grated

Pasta with Ricotta Cheese

Fill a large saucepan ¾ full with water, bring to the boil, then add pasta and cook until just tender. Reserve some of the hot water and drain the pasta well. Sauté the mushrooms in a little oil, add salt, pepper, parsley and soya mince. In a serving bowl, mash the Ricotta cheese with a fork and add 2 tablespoons of hot pasta water to dilute. Add fried mushrooms, soya mince and cooked pasta, and mix well.

Sprinkle with cheese and serve hot.

SERVES 4-6.

500 g (1 lb) penne pasta
boiling water, with a pinch of salt and
  a few drops of oil
250 g (8 oz) mushrooms, chopped
2 tbs oil
salt and pepper, to taste
2 tbs fresh parsley, chopped
125 g (4 oz) soya mince
155 g (5 oz) Ricotta cheese
90 g (3 oz) Parmesan cheese, grated

Pasta with Tofu and Vegetables

Fill a large saucepan ¾ full with water, bring to the boil, then add pasta and cook until just tender. Drain well. Heat the oil in a pan. Fry the corn and peas for 5-10 minutes. Add the blended tomatoes and purée. The consistency should not be runny, but if it gets too thick, add a little water and cook for 10 more minutes. Add salt and pepper. Cut the tofu into small chunks and deep fry for 2-3 minutes.

Mix the pasta with the tomato sauce and fried tofu, adding extra water if necessary. Sprinkle with parsley.

Pasta should be not overcooked.

SERVES 5-6.

500 g (1 lb) pasta, cooked and drained
boiling water, with a pinch of salt and
  a few drops of oil
4 tbs oil
125 g (4 oz) frozen corn
125 g (4 oz) frozen peas
440 g (14 oz) canned tomatoes
2-3 tbs tomato purée
250 ml (8 fl oz) water
salt and pepper, to taste
315 g (10 oz) tofu
oil, for deep frying
handful of fresh parsley, chopped

Peas and Potato Curry (Opposite)

Put the oil into a fairly large saucepan, over a medium heat. When the oil is hot, add mustard seeds and allow them to pop. Add the cumin seeds and allow them to brown. Add the tomatoes and cook for 5 minutes stirring gently. Season with the spices. Mix until the spices have thoroughly blended. Add the vegetables and water, cover the saucepan and cook on a low heat until the potatoes are tender.

Sprinkle with fresh coriander leaves.

Serve with Cucumber Raita (page 40), Naan Bread (page 182) and Pappadams.

SERVES 4.

1 tbs oil
½ tsp mustard seeds
1 tsp cumin seeds
3 medium size tomatoes, diced
½ tsp salt, to taste
2 tbs coriander seeds, ground
½ tsp turmeric
1 chilli, seeded and chopped (optional)
1 tbs fresh ginger, crushed
2-3 medium potatoes, diced
125 g (4 oz) frozen peas
300 ml (½ pint) water
fresh coriander leaves, chopped

Pasties

Mix the flour, salt and oil in a bowl. Rub with fingertips until the mixture resembles breadcrumbs. Add water to make a soft dough.

Heat the oil in a saucepan, add all the vegetables, soya chunks and seasonings and cook until tender, adding a little water if necessary.

Roll the pastry out to 5 mm (¼ in) thick. Cut into rounds, approximately saucer size. Place 1 tablespoon of filling on each round and fold the pastry over, wetting the edges to make it stick. Brush the top with milk, place on a greased baking tray and bake at 180°C/350°F/Gas Mark 4 for 30 minutes or until golden brown.

Serve with Tomato Sauce (page 89).

MAKES 10-12 PASTIES.

PASTRY
185 g (6 oz) wholemeal flour
pinch of salt
3 tbs oil
300 ml (½ pint) cold water
milk, for glazing

FILLING
2 tbs oil
2 large potatoes, cubed small
250 g (8 oz) carrot, cubed small
125 g (4 oz) mushrooms, chopped
125 g (4 oz) soya chunks, boiled,
  drained and chopped
salt and pepper, to taste
1 tsp dried mixed herbs
1 tsp fennel seeds

Potato and Tomato Bake

Slice the potatoes and tomatoes thickly. Alternate the vegetables in a casserole dish, sprinkling each layer with herbs, salt, pepper and butter or margarine. Finish with a layer of tomatoes. Pour milk over the vegetables, cover the dish and bake in the oven at 180°C/350°F/Gas Mark 4 for about 30 minutes. Remove the cover for last 5 minutes of cooking time. Sprinkle with parsley.

SERVES 4-5.

500 g (1 lb) potatoes, peeled
750 g (1½ lb) tomatoes, skinned
1 tsp dried oregano
1 tsp dried thyme
salt and pepper, to taste
15 g (½ oz) butter OR margarine
250 ml (8 fl oz) milk
2 tbs fresh parsley, chopped

Potato Burgers

Boil and mash the potatoes. Fry the vegetables in 2 tablespoons of oil until just tender. Add the seasoning and herbs, and mix the vegetables with the mashed potatoes. Form into burger shapes, place on a greased tray and bake at 180°C/350°F/Gas Mark 4 until slightly brown or shallow fry for 2 minutes. Top the burgers with cheese and bake for another 10-20 minutes.

**Vegetables can be varied according to choice.
Serve with rolls and a salad.**

MAKES 25 BURGERS.

500 g (1 lb) potatoes, peeled and quartered
250 g (8 oz) mixed frozen vegetables
125 g (4 oz) mushrooms, finely chopped
60 g (2 oz) cabbage, finely chopped
60 g (2 oz) spinach, finely chopped
2 tbs oil
salt and pepper, to taste
herbs, to taste (optional)
oil, for frying
220 g (7 oz) mild Cheddar cheese, grated

Potato Curry

Heat the oil in a saucepan, add cumin seeds, mustard seeds and asafoetida. When the seeds pop, add the potatoes, salt and turmeric. Toss the potatoes in the pan, cover and cook for a few minutes on a very low heat, stirring from time to time to prevent sticking and burning. When the potatoes are half cooked, add tomatoes, ground coriander, ground cumin, chilli and warm water. Cover the pan and cook until the potatoes are soft and well cooked. Add the lemon juice, simmer for 1 minute and turn off the heat. Garnish with chopped coriander leaves and serve hot with chapatis, puri, bread or rice.

The amount of water can be increased for more sauce or reduced as required. You can even mash a few pieces of potato and add them to thicken the sauce.

SERVES 4.

2½ – 3 tbs oil
½ tsp cumin seeds
½ tsp mustard seeds
pinch of asafoetida (hing) (optional)
500 g (1 lb) potatoes, peeled and diced
salt, to taste
½ tsp turmeric, ground
185 g (6 oz) tomatoes, chopped
1 tbs coriander seeds, ground
1 tbs cumin seeds, ground
1 chilli, chopped (optional)
150 ml (¼ pint) warm water
1 tsp lemon juice
coriander leaves, chopped

PIZZA (Opposite)

Plain Pizza Base

Mix the flour, salt and oil with enough water to make a manageable dough. Roll out to about 5 mm (¼ in) thick and press the pastry onto an oiled baking tray.

Mix all the sauce ingredients and place a couple of scoops on the pastry.

Arrange the vegetables and cheese on top. Bake at 200°C/400°F/Gas Mark 6 for 20 minutes.

Serve with a salad.

SERVES 6-8.

BASE
500 g (1 lb) self-raising flour
pinch of salt
4 tbs oil
water, to mix

SAUCE
440 g (14 oz) canned tomatoes
2 tbs oil
salt and pepper, to taste
1-2 tsp oregano
1 tsp sugar

TOPPING
500 g (1 lb) mushrooms, finely chopped
1-2 green peppers, finely chopped
60 g (2 oz) Mozzarella cheese

Yeast Pizza Base

Sift the flour and sugar into a mixing bowl, then add the yeast. Add water and mix to form a dough. Turn onto a lightly floured surface and knead for 5 minutes. Roll out to a 5 mm (¼ in) thick round pizza shape and place the dough on a non-stick baking tray. Brush the top of the dough with a small amount of oil. Cover and leave to rise for about 30 minutes, while you make the sauce.

Heat 4 tablespoons of oil in a saucepan and add the red pepper. Cover and cook for 5 minutes. Add the tomatoes and mash with a fork or potato masher. Season with salt and pepper. Leave to cook uncovered for 20 minutes until the mixture thickens.

Sprinkle the pizza base with oregano, then spread the cooked tomato mixture over it. Arrange the olives on top and finish with cheese.

Bake in a hot oven at 375°F/190°C/Gas Mark 5 for 25-30 minutes, until the cheese has melted and the base is cooked.

Serve with a salad.

SERVES 2-4.

BASE
250 g (8 oz) wholemeal flour
1 tsp sugar
15 g (½ oz) dried yeast
150 ml (¼ pint) water
oil

SAUCE
4 tbs oil
½ red pepper, diced
440 g (14 oz) canned tomatoes
salt and pepper, to taste
1 tsp oregano

TOPPING
olives
125 g (4 oz) Mozzarella cheese, grated

Yoghurt Pizza Base

Mix the flour and oil. Stir in the yoghurt and form a soft dough. Cover and leave on one side until it is twice the size.

Meanwhile, make the sauce by mixing the oil, tomatoes, herbs and seasonings together.

Punch dough down, roll it out and press it into 2 large, greased flan or pizza trays. Spread the sauce over the dough. Garnish with olives, mushrooms and cheese.

Bake at 220°C/425°F/Gas Mark 7 for 20-25 minutes.

Serve with a salad.

SERVES 6.

BASE
375 g (12 oz) self-raising flour
100 ml (3 fl oz) oil
4 tbs yoghurt

SAUCE
4 tbs oil
410 g (13 oz) canned tomatoes
2 tbs oregano
1 tbs basil
salt and pepper, to taste

TOPPING
black olives, stoned and sliced
250 g (8 oz) mushrooms, sliced
155 g (5 oz) Mozzarella cheese, grated

Potato Pie

Sift the flour, baking powder and salt together into a mixing bowl. Melt the butter or margarine, pour into the flour and mix well. Add enough water to make a lumpy dough. Roll out the pastry and line a flan dish.

Bake at 200°C/400°F/Gas Mark 6 for approximately 10 minutes or until golden brown.

Add the cream to the potatoes. Cook the spinach in a little oil, then mix with the potatoes and add salt and pepper. Spoon the mixture onto the half-cooked pastry base. Sprinkle sesame seeds on top and bake for a further 15-20 minutes.

SERVES 6.

PASTRY
250 g (8 oz) plain flour
1 tsp baking powder
½ tsp salt
125 g (4 oz) butter OR margarine
cold water, to mix

FILLING
125 ml (4 fl oz) single cream
4 medium sized potatoes, boiled and mashed
250 g (8 oz) spinach, chopped
1 tbs of oil
salt and pepper, to taste
1 tbs sesame seeds

Pumpkin Pie

Knead the flour, salt and butter or margarine into a dough, adding a little water, to form hard base; add lemon juice. Roll out to the size of a baking dish. Bake at 160°C/325°F/Gas Mark 3 for 20 minutes.

Melt half the butter or margarine and fry the cashew nuts until golden. Peel the pumpkin, remove the seeds and chop into squares. Microwave or steam until tender. Purée or mash with the remaining butter or margarine, then add the cashew nuts, tomato purée, spices, herbs, honey, cream or milk and cornflour. Heat until nearly boiling, then pour onto the base. Top with cheese and herbs.

Bake at 200°C/400°F/Gas Mark 6 until golden brown on top.

SERVES 4-5.

BASE
375 g (12 oz) plain flour
1 tsp salt
220 g (7 oz) butter OR margarine
water, to mix
3 tbs lemon juice
FILLING
90 g (3 oz) butter OR margarine
60 g (2 oz) cashew nuts
1 large pumpkin
2 tbs tomato purée
1 tbs black pepper, crushed
pinch of salt
½ tbs cardamom, crushed
½ tbs cumin, roasted and crushed
1 tbs oregano
1 tbs basil
1 tbs honey
300 ml (½ pint) cream OR milk
1 tbs cornflour
TOPPING
125 g (4 oz) Cheddar cheese, grated
½ tbs oregano
½ tbs mixed herbs

Rice and Vegetable Bake

Sauté vegetables in oil for 10 minutes. Combine vegetables, cooked rice, oats and soya sauce and mix thoroughly. Add a little warm water if too dry. Transfer to a greased baking tray or tin. Sprinkle sunflower seeds on top and bake at 200°C/400°F/Gas Mark 6 for 45 minutes.

Serve with a sauce of your choice (page 88-89).

SERVES 4-5.

2-3 medium sized carrots, diced
½ cauliflower, diced
2 tbs oil
250 g (8 oz) brown rice, cooked
125 g (4 oz) rolled oats
2 tbs soya sauce
30 g (1 oz) sunflower seeds

Rice with French Beans

Combine beans, cooked rice, oats, and soya sauce and mix thoroughly. Add a little warm water if too dry. Transfer to a greased baking tray or tin. Sprinkle sunflower seeds on top and bake at 200°C/400°F/Gas Mark 6 for 45 minutes.

Serve with a sauce of your choice (page 88-89).

SERVES 4-5.

170 g (6 oz) French beans, chopped
  and boiled
2 tbs oil
250 g (8 oz) brown rice, cooked
125 g (4 oz) rolled oats
2 tbs soya sauce
30 g (1 oz) sunflower seeds

Savoury Pancakes

Mix all the dry ingredients together and beat with a fork for 5 minutes, with enough water or milk to make the consistency of butter. Heat the oil in a heavy frying pan. Pour in a spoonful of batter, and cook each pancake on both sides for 4-6 minutes.

Fry all the filling ingredients in oil. Cook until all the vegetables are soft. Allow to cool slightly, then roll the filling into the pancake.

Serve hot with Tomato Sauce (page 89).

SERVES 6.

PANCAKE
250 g (8 oz) self-raising flour
1 tsp salt
water OR milk
oil, for frying

FILLING
1 carrot, grated
60 g (2 oz) mushrooms, chopped
salt and pepper, to taste
1 tbs fresh parsley, chopped
1-2 tbs oil

Spaghetti Bolognese (Opposite)

Fill a large saucepan ¾ full with water, bring to the boil, then add macaroni and cook until just tender. Drain well. Prepare the sauce by heating the oil in a saucepan and frying the mushrooms and soya mince for a few minutes. Add the liquidised tomatoes, salt, pepper and basil and simmer for 10 minutes. The sauce should be fairly thick. To serve, put spaghetti on a plate, pour some sauce over and sprinkle cheese on top.

SERVES 4.

500 g (1 lb) spaghetti
boiling water, with a pinch of salt and
  a few drops of oil
2 tbs olive oil
250 g (8 oz) mushrooms, sliced
90 g (3 oz) soya mince
440 g (14 oz) canned tomatoes, liquidised
salt and pepper, to taste
2 tbs dried basil OR handful of fresh basil
125 g (4 oz) Parmesan cheese, grated

Spaghetti Bolognese and Soya Mince Bake

Mix cooked spaghetti with Bolognese sauce. Place in an ovenproof dish and pour cheese sauce on top. Sprinkle with cheese and fresh basil, and bake in the oven at 200°C/400°F/Gas Mark 6 for 15 minutes until golden brown.

SERVES 2-4.

sauce ingredients as Spaghetti Bolognese (page 70)
½ quantity Cheese Sauce (page 89)
125 g (4 oz) Parmesan cheese, grated
2 tbs dried basil OR handful of fresh basil

Soya Burgers

Place the soya mince in a bowl and cover with boiling water. Leave to stand for 10 minutes or until all the water is absorbed. Then add the carrot, potatoes, peanut butter or tahini, peppers, cabbage, salt and pepper. Add herbs or spices of your choice. Mix to make a firm dough. If the dough is too soft, add a little flour. Form a small amount of dough into a burger shape and fry in a shallow frying pan until brown on both sides, or brush with oil and bake in the oven at 190°C/375°F/Gas Mark 5 until brown.

Serve with Tomato Sauce (page 89) and a salad.

SERVES 10-12.

125 g (4 oz) soya mince
1 carrot, grated
2-3 medium sized potatoes, cooked, peeled
  and mashed
60 g (2 oz) melted peanut butter OR tahini
1-2 peppers, chopped
60 g (2 oz) cabbage, grated
salt and pepper, to taste
1-2 tsp herbs OR spices, (optional)
oil, for frying

Spicy Burgers

Rinse and drain the beans. Cover them with cold water in a pan. Bring the water to the boil and continue boiling rapidly for 10 minutes. Drain and cover with fresh water, bring to the boil again, then cover and simmer for 20-25 minutes until tender. Drain well and mash. Gently fry the green pepper, celery, walnuts and carrots in oil for 3-4 minutes. Add the soya sauce, chillies and parsley and mix together well. Shape into 8 balls. Flatten to about 1 cm (½ in) thick. Coat the burgers with breadcrumbs and fry in hot shallow oil for 4 minutes on each side.

Serve with Tomato Sauce (page 89) and a salad.

MAKES 8 BURGERS.

250 g (8 oz) black eyed beans, soaked overnight
cold water, to cover
1 green pepper, finely chopped
1 stick celery, finely chopped
60 g (2 oz) walnuts, chopped
2 carrots, grated
2 tbs oil
1 tbs soya sauce
2 chillies
2 tbs parsley, chopped
60 g (2 oz) wholemeal breadcrumbs, mixed
  with 1 tsp dried/fresh herbs
oil, for frying

Spinach Flan

Set the oven to 180°C/350°F/Gas Mark 4. Place a 20 cm (8 in) flan ring on a baking sheet. Roll out the pastry on a lightly floured surface and use to line the flan ring. Prick the base lightly with a fork. Melt the butter or margarine in a medium sized saucepan. Add the spinach, cover and cook very gently for 7 minutes, stirring occasionally. Add salt and pepper. Drain very thoroughly. Gently stir the yoghurt and cheese together and season well. Spread the drained spinach over the base of the flan; cover with the cheese mixture.

Bake in the oven for 25-30 minutes until set and lightly browned.

Serve with a salad.

SERVES 4-5.

250 g (8 oz) Shortcrust Pastry (see Breads)
flour, for rolling
30 g (1 oz) butter OR margarine
1 kg (2 lb) spinach, chopped
salt and pepper, to taste
150 ml (¼ pint) plain yoghurt
185 g (6 oz) Cheddar cheese, grated

Spinach Pie (Opposite)

Heat half the oil in a saucepan. Add the spinach, stir, cover and cook for 10-15 minutes. Fry the mushrooms separately with the remainder of the oil. Drain the spinach (keep the water for a healthy vitamin enriched juice or stock) and mix with salt, pepper, fried mushrooms and cottage cheese. Sift the flour and salt into a bowl. Rub in the margarine and add water to make a soft dough. Roll the dough out to 1 cm (½ in) thick on a floured board. Grease a 25 x 30 cm (10 x 12 in) ovenproof dish. Place the pastry in the dish and spread the spinach mixture evenly on top. Sprinkle with grated cheese.

Bake on the middle shelf at 190°C/375°F/Gas Mark 5 for 20 minutes or until golden brown.

Serve with baked potatoes and a salad.

SERVES 4.

FILLING
3 tbs oil
1.5 kg (3 lb) fresh spinach, washed and chopped
250 g (8 oz) mushrooms, sliced
salt and pepper, to taste
1 kg (2 lb) plain cottage cheese
fresh parsley, chopped
90 g (3 oz) Cheddar cheese, grated
handful sesame seeds for decoration

PASTRY
250 g (8 oz) self-raising flour
pinch of salt
4 oz margarine
cold water, to mix

Stir-Fried Rice

Heat the oil in a pan, add ginger and cabbage and fry until slightly brown. Add water or vegetable stock, orange rind, sultanas or raisins, orange juice, lemon juice, salt and pepper and simmer for 15 minutes. Drain the rice, add to the pan and cook until the rice is tender. Garnish with mint or coriander leaves.

SERVES 4-5.

3 tbs oil
1 tsp fresh ginger, crushed
125 ml (4 fl oz) white cabbage, finely shredded
900 ml (1½ pints) water OR vegetable stock
rind of ½ orange, grated
60 g (2 oz) sultanas OR raisins
1 tbs orange juice
1 tbs lemon juice
salt and pepper, to taste
250 g (8 oz) white rice, soaked
handful of fresh mint OR coriander leaves, chopped

Stuffed Aubergines

Set the oven to 190°C/375°F/Gas Mark 5. Prick the aubergines all over, cut in half and place the cut side down on a greased baking sheet. Bake for 30 minutes. Heat the oil in a pan and fry the celery gently for 5 minutes. Add the mushrooms and cook, stirring for 3 minutes. Stir in rice, walnuts, tomato purée, parsley and seasoning. Scoop the flesh from the aubergines, without breaking the skins. Chop the flesh finely and mix with the fried mixture. Pile back into the aubergine skins, sprinkle with cheese and place under a hot grill until heated thoroughly.

Serve immediately with a salad.

SERVES 4.

2 large aubergines (eggplant)
2-3 tbs oil
3 sticks celery, finely chopped
220 g (7 oz) mushrooms, thinly sliced
6 tbs rice, cooked
60 g (2 oz) walnuts, coarsely chopped
1 tsp tomato purée
2 tbs fresh parsley, chopped
salt and pepper, to taste
75 g (2½ oz) Cheddar cheese, grated

Stuffed Cabbage

Boil the cabbage leaves for 5 minutes in salted water. Keep the water (stock) and put the cabbage aside to drain. Mix the remaining ingredients together and form into 6 balls. Wrap each ball with a cabbage leaf, secure with a cocktail stick and place in an ovenproof dish. Cover with a little of the stock from the cabbage.

Bake in the oven at 200°C/400°F/Gas Mark 6 for 30-40 minutes.

Adding a little cornflour can thicken the stock.

SERVES 6.

6 large Savoy cabbage leaves
boiling water, with a pinch of salt
125 g (4 oz) brown rice, cooked
60 g (2 oz) mushrooms, chopped
125 g (4 oz) soya mince
salt and pepper, to taste
2 tsp oil

Vegetable Rolls

Boil all the vegetables together until just soft, then mash. Melt the butter or margarine in a saucepan. Add flour and then gradually add the milk to make a smooth white sauce. Mix the sauce with the mashed vegetables and add the cheese and oatmeal to make a firm dough. Shape the dough into oval shaped rolls. Deep fry in hot oil for 8 minutes, turning constantly until golden brown all over.

Serve with a salad.

SERVES 6.

1 small cauliflower, cubed
2 carrots, cubed
2 potatoes, cubed
125 g (4 oz) courgettes (zucchini), cubed
125 g (4 oz) green peas
60 g (2 oz) butter OR margarine
60 g (2 oz) flour
250 ml (8 fl oz) milk
125 g (4 oz) mild Cheddar cheese, grated
125 g (4 oz) oatmeal
oil, for deep frying

Stir-Fried Vegetables (Opposite)

Heat the oil and ginger in a wok. Individually add vegetables and stir-fry quickly for 5-10 minutes. Mix all the vegetables together. Stir in soya sauce and sesame oil. Season and serve immediately.

Serve with noodles or rice.

SERVES 6.

3 tbs oil
2 tbs fresh ginger
125 g (4 oz) broccoli, broken into florets
125 g (4 oz) cauliflower, broken into florets
250 g (8 oz) baby sweetcorn, cut in two
125 g (4 oz) cabbage, shredded
125 g (4 oz) carrots, cut into matchsticks
125 g (4 oz) mushrooms, sliced
2 red peppers, cut into strips
2 green peppers, cut into strips
125 g (4 oz) hard tofu, cut into sticks
soya sauce, to taste
1 tsp sesame oil
pepper, to taste

Vegetable Flans

To make pastry, put the flours and margarine into a mixing bowl and rub lightly together with fingertips until the mixture resembles breadcrumbs. Add enough water to make a firm dough. Roll out the pastry on a lightly floured surface and line six 14 cm (5 ½ in) individual flan tins. Prick the base of each flan and chill for ½ hour. Line each flan with greaseproof paper or aluminium foil and fill with dried beans. Bake blind in a hot oven at 200°C/400°F/Gas Mark 6 for 10 minutes. Remove the beans and paper or foil. Keep the beans to use again.

Heat the oil, gently fry the vegetables, herbs and seasoning, then cook for 15 minutes. Spoon the mixture into the flan cases. Beat the yoghurt, cornflour and milk together, add the cream and cheese and pour over the filling.

Bake the flans at 190°C/375°F/Gas Mark 5 for 15-20 minutes or until set.

MAKES 6 FLANS.

PASTRY
315 g (10 oz) wholewheat flour
185 g (6 oz) plain flour
185 g (6 oz) margarine
cold water, to mix
dried beans, for baking blind

FILLING
1 tbs oil
1 red pepper, sliced
185 g (6 oz) courgettes (zucchini), thinly sliced
4 tomatoes, skinned and chopped
1 tbs fresh marjoram, chopped
1 tbs fresh basil, chopped
salt and pepper, to taste
1 tbs plain yoghurt
1 tbs cornflour
1 tbs milk
100 ml (3 fl oz) single cream
60 g (2 oz) Cheddar cheese, grated

Stuffed Peppers (Opposite)

Cut the peppers in half and discard the seeds. Place the peppers in boiling water, remove the pan from the heat and leave the peppers in water with the lid on for at least 5 minutes, then drain. Fry the soya mince in oil. Combine the soya mince, rice, salt, pepper, sesame oil, soya sauce and coriander leaves. Fill each pepper with this mixture. Place the peppers on a baking tray, sprinkle cheese on top and bake at 325°F/160°C/Gas Mark 3 for 20-30 minutes.

Serve with salad.

SERVES 4.

3 peppers (green, red or yellow)
60 g (2 oz) soya mince
1 tbs oil
125 g (4 oz) brown rice, cooked
salt and pepper, to taste
½ tsp sesame oil
2 tbs soya sauce
60 g (2 oz) fresh coriander leaves
125 g (4 oz) Cheddar cheese, grated

Vegetable Pancakes

Whisk together self-raising flour, milk, salt and pepper until the batter becomes smooth and creamy. Leave to stand for 5 minutes, then add all the ingredients except the oil.

Heat 1 tablespoon of oil in a frying pan, spread the pancake mixture evenly over the pan and allow it to fry on a low heat until golden, then turn it over to cook the other side. A few drops of oil can be added to the side of the pan to prevent sticking.

Serve hot.

MAKES 6-8.

250 g (8 oz) self-raising flour
milk, to mix
salt and pepper, to taste
60 g (2 oz) cabbage, finely shredded
60 g (2 oz) frozen corn
2 medium-sized tomatoes, diced
1 green pepper, diced small
1 tsp ginger, grated
herbs, of your choice
oil, for frying

Tagliatelle with Mushrooms (Opposite)

Cook the tagliatelle in boiling water for 10-15 minutes, or according to the instructions on the packet. Meanwhile, fry the mushrooms in butter and add salt and pepper. Drain the tagliatelle and place in a bowl, mixing in the cheese, double cream and fried mushrooms. Sprinkle with parsley and serve immediately.

Optional: add basil and paprika to the cream.

SERVES 4-5.

1.2-1.8 l (2-3 pints) boiling water, with a pinch of salt and a few drops of oil
500 g (1 lb) tagliatelle
250 g (8 oz) mushrooms, chopped
2 tsp butter
salt and pepper, to taste
90 g (3 oz) Parmesan cheese, grated
250 ml (8 fl oz) double cream
2 tbs fresh parsley, chopped

Vegetable Pie

Peel the potatoes and cut the large ones in half. Cover with cold water and 2 teaspoons of salt, bring to the boil and cook for 10 minutes, then drain and slice. Melt 60 g (2 oz) of butter or margarine in a medium sized saucepan and sauté the carrots. Add Brussels sprouts and 3 tablespoons water. Cover and cook gently for 2 minutes, stirring occasionally. Stir in the sage, salt and pepper. Stir in the flour, and cook gently for 2 minutes. Gradually stir in the milk and cook gently for 3 minutes or until thickened. Remove the pan from the heat. Arrange half the potatoes on the base of an ovenproof dish, and cover with the sprout and carrot mixture. Arrange the remainder of the potatoes over the top. Melt the remaining butter or margarine and brush over the potatoes. Spread the cheese on top. Grill gently until brown.

SERVES 4-6.

1 kg (2 lb) potatoes
cold water, to cover
2 tsp salt
90 g (3 oz) butter OR margarine
375 g (12 oz) carrots, sliced round
375 g (12 oz) Brussels sprouts, halved
3 tbs water
¼ tsp dried sage
salt and pepper, to taste
30 g (1 oz) flour
150 ml (¼ pint) milk
90 g (3 oz) mild Cheddar cheese, grated for topping

Tofu Flan

Fry the vegetables in the oil for 5 minutes, then set aside. Mix the tofu with the fried vegetables, walnuts, salt, vinegar and herbs.

Sift the flour and salt, make a well in the middle for the oil. Rub the oil lightly into the flour until it feels like wet sand. Add a little water; mix together, then press into a 25 x 30 cm (10 x 12 in) flan tin. Cover with tofu mixture, decorate with tomato and bake at 200°C/400°F/Gas Mark 6 for 25-30 minutes.

SERVES 4-5.

FILLING
1 large carrot, diced
440 g (14 oz) broccoli, chopped
2 tbs oil
875 g (¾ lb) tofu, drained and mashed
60 g (2 oz) walnuts, chopped
1½ tsp salt
5 tsp cider vinegar
1 tsp herbs (optional)
1 large tomato, sliced

PASTRY
625 g (1¼ lb) plain flour
pinch of salt
180 ml (6 fl oz) oil
cold water, to mix

Vegetable Rice

Rinse and drain the rice. Heat 1 teaspoon of the oil in a pan, add the rice and cook for 2 minutes, stirring continuously on a low heat. Add hot water and bring to the boil. Reduce the heat and simmer for 40-45 minutes, adding more water if necessary.

Heat the remaining oil in another pan, add red pepper and mushrooms and fry for 3 minutes. Stir in the cooked rice and flaked almonds, adjust seasoning to taste and sprinkle with parsley and cheese.

SERVES 3-4.

250 g (8 oz) brown rice
3 tsp oil
600 ml (1 pint) hot water
1 red pepper, chopped
440 g (14 oz) mushrooms, quartered
60 g (2 oz) almonds, flaked
salt and pepper, to taste
1 tbs parsley
90 g (3 oz) Parmesan cheese, grated for topping

Vegetarian Shepherd's Pie

Peel the potatoes. Put them in a saucepan, cover with boiling water, cover and boil until just soft. Meanwhile to prepare the filling, heat 2 tablespoons of oil in a wok or frying pan, add asafoetida and cabbage and fry until slightly brown. Then add carrots, mushrooms and sweetcorn. Fry together for 10 more minutes. Place the filling in an ovenproof dish. Fry the soya mince in 2 tablespoons of oil for 5 minutes and then add to the filling. Put the blended tomatoes in the wok with 1 tablespoon of oil. Bring to the boil for 5 minutes and add mixed herbs, salt, pepper and parsley. Add the tomato sauce to the filling and mix well. Add more salt and pepper if necessary.

Drain and mash the potatoes. Add butter, milk, a handful of the grated cheese, parsley, salt and pepper and mix until creamy. Spread the mashed potatoes over the filling. Sprinkle with the remaining cheese and bake in the oven at 200°C/400°F/Gas Mark 6 for 20 minutes until golden brown.

SERVES 3-4.

500 g (1 lb) potatoes
boiling water, with a pinch of salt
60 g (2 oz) butter
180 ml (6 fl oz) milk
125 g (4 oz) mild Cheddar cheese, grated
fresh parsley, chopped
salt and pepper, to taste

FILLING
5 tbs vegetable oil
½ tsp asafoetida (hing)
125 g (4 oz) cabbage
250 g (8 oz) grated carrots
500 g (1 lb) chopped mushrooms
250 g (8 oz) canned or frozen sweetcorn
250 g (8 oz) soya mince
220 g (7 oz) canned tomatoes, blended
1 tsp mixed herbs
salt and pepper, to taste
fresh parsley, chopped

Walnut Cheese Burgers

Fry the mushrooms and cabbage in a tablespoon of oil or butter. Mix all the ingredients together to form into a solid dough. Add a little milk if needed. Shape into balls and flatten into burger shapes. Fry in oil in a shallow pan until brown.

Serve with Tomato Sauce (page 89) and a salad.

MAKES 6-8 BURGERS.

60 g (2 oz) mushrooms, finely chopped
60 g (2 oz) cabbage, shredded
1 tbs oil OR butter
185 g (6 oz) walnuts, ground
60 g (2 oz) breadcrumbs
125 g (4 oz) cheese
salt and pepper, to taste
1 tbs tomato purée
handful of fresh parsley, chopped
2 tbs milk
60 g (2 oz) soya mince
oil, for frying

Sauces
& Chutneys

Brown Gravy
Cashew Gravy
Mushroom Gravy
Yoghurt Mint Sauce
Sweet and Sour Sauce
Tomato Sauce
White Sauce
Cheese Sauce
Parsley Sauce
Chutney for Pakoras
Green Chilli Chutney
Red Pepper Chutney
Red Plum Chutney
Tomato Chutney

Brown Gravy

Mix water, soya sauce and cornflour in a saucepan. Stir until the cornflour dissolves. Place over a low heat and stir gently and continuously until the mixture thickens.

Serve on stir-fried vegetables.

125 ml (4 fl oz) water
60 ml (2 fl oz) dark soya sauce
2-3 tbs cornflour

Cashew Gravy

Blend all ingredients in a blender, then heat in a saucepan, stirring with a wooden spoon until thick and almost boiling.

Serve on pies or vegetables.

500 g (1 lb) cashew nuts, ground
1.2 l (2 pints) milk OR water
5 tsp arrowroot
1 tsp celery seed, ground
1 tsp asafoetida (hing)
2 tbs olive oil
1 tsp salt

Mushroom Gravy

Sauté mushrooms in butter or oil. Blend cornstarch, water and soya sauce together. Combine all ingredients in a pan and simmer, stirring constantly until thick and almost boiling. Add pepper.

Serve on mashed potatoes or steamed, boiled or stir-fried vegetables.

60 g (2 oz) mushrooms, sliced
1 tbs butter OR oil
2 tbs cornstarch
250 ml (8 fl oz) water
2 tbs soya sauce
pepper, to taste

Yoghurt Mint Sauce

Mix all the ingredients together and serve.

125 ml (4 fl oz) plain yoghurt
2 tbs mint, chopped
1 small green chilli, de-seeded and
  finely chopped
salt, to taste

Sweet and Sour Sauce

Stir all the ingredients together over a low heat until the sauce boils and thickens.

3 tbs cider vinegar
3 tbs tomato purée
250 ml (8 fl oz) water
4–5 tbs sugar
pinch of asafoetida (hing)
1–2 tbs cornflour
1 tbs oil

Tomato Sauce

Heat the oil in a small pan with a pinch of asafoetida. Add the tomato purée, water, lemon juice and cornflour. Keep stirring until the sauce thickens. Add the sugar, salt and pepper.

Serve on chips and burgers or any savoury dishes.

1 tbs vegetable oil
pinch of asafoetida (hing)
2–3 tbs tomato purée
250 ml (8 fl oz) water
2–3 tbs lemon juice
1–2 tbs cornflour
1 tbs sugar
salt and pepper, to taste

White Sauce

Melt the butter or margarine in a saucepan and add the flour or cornflour. Cook for 2–3 minutes, blending together well with a whisk or wooden spoon. Add the vegetable stock or water and the milk. Heat, stirring at first to ensure that there are no lumps. Cook until the sauce is of a smooth and even consistency. Season with salt, pepper and nutmeg. For a thinner sauce, add more liquid.
OR
Mix all the ingredients in a saucepan and put on a low heat. Stir slowly until well mixed. After 5 minutes, turn up the heat to thicken the sauce.

Variations:
1. *Cheese Sauce* : **as White Sauce, adding 90 g (3 oz) grated cheese after the sauce is cooked. Mild, mature or strong Cheddar can be used, depending upon taste.**
2. *Parsley Sauce* : **as White Sauce, adding 30 g (1 oz) chopped fresh parsley.**

30 g (1 oz) butter OR margarine
30 g (1 oz) plain flour OR cornflour
150 ml (¼ pint) vegetable stock OR water
300 ml (½ pint) milk
salt and pepper, to taste
pinch of nutmeg, ground

Sa

Chutney for Pakoras

Mix all the ingredients together and liquidise. Garnish with coriander.

1 small carrot, chopped
1 cucumber, small piece about 7.5 cm (3 in) long
3 medium tomatoes
3 green chillies
1 small raw mango OR juice of ½ lemon
2 tsp cumin seeds
salt and sugar, to taste
2 tbs fresh coriander leaves, for garnish

Green Chilli Chutney

Wash the coriander or parsley leaves thoroughly. Put everything into a blender and blend.

bunch of coriander leaves OR parsley, chopped
2-3 green chillies, chopped
½ apple, peeled and cubed
¼ tsp sugar
juice of ½ lemon
1 level tsp salt

Red Pepper Chutney

Remove the seeds from the red pepper and chop coarsely. Blend all the ingredients together, except the coriander leaves. Garnish with chopped coriander leaves.

1 red pepper
3 green chillies
2 tsp cumin seeds
juice of ½ lemon
salt, to taste
sugar, to taste
1 tbs coriander leaves, chopped

Red Plum Chutney

Put plums and apples into a large saucepan, then add the remaining ingredients. Bring slowly to the boil, stirring continuously, until the sugar has dissolved. Increase the heat and simmer, uncovered, until the chutney is thick and mushy – about 75 minutes. Store in an airtight container.

1 kg (2 lb) red plums, halved and stoned
500 g (1 lb) cooking apples, peeled, cored and chopped
500 g (1 lb) demerara sugar
2 tsp ginger
1 tsp mixed spice
600 ml (1 pint) pickling vinegar

Tomato Chutney

Peel tomatoes, slice and put into a bowl with a sprinkling of salt. Leave to stand overnight.

Next day, put tomatoes in a pan. Peel and slice the apples. and add them to the pan with vinegar, sugar, cayenne, cloves and cinnamon. Bring to a boil and simmer, stirring, until the sugar has dissolved and the fruit and vegetables are tender. Pour into warmed, dry jars and add one or two green chillies to each jar. Allow to cool, cover tightly and store.

500 g (1 lb) tomatoes, chopped
1 tbs salt
3 large Bramley apples
300 ml (½ pint) cider vinegar
500 g (1 lb) sugar
1 tsp cayenne pepper
1 tsp cloves, ground
1 tsp cinnamon, ground
green chillies (optional)

Side Dishes

Baked Beans
Green Beans with Flaked Almonds
Broccoli with Ginger Sauce
Broccoli with Walnuts
Dhokra
Brussels Sprouts au Gratin
Peperonata
Hungarian Courgettes
Chick Pea and Coriander Patties
Quick Pilau Rice
Jamaican Rice
Crunchy Cabbage
Potato Pancakes
Mushrooms and Tomatoes
Fried Aubergine
Roast Potatoes
Lentil Rolls
Fried Rice
Roast Parsnips
Savoury Rice
Fried Rice Balls
Savoury Vermicelli
Green Beans and Tomato
Saffron Rice
Stuffed Mushrooms
Okra with Tomatoes
Paneer in Green Masala
Pasta with Herbs
Potato Balls

Baked Beans (Opposite)

Drain and rinse the soaked beans. Cook for 1 hour in plenty of water until soft and tender or pressure cook (make sure the water covers the beans) for 15 minutes, and then drain. Meanwhile, blend tomatoes and purée together. Heat the oil in a pan and add blended tomatoes. Add salt, pepper, vinegar and sugar and simmer for 10-15 minutes. Add the drained beans to the sauce and simmer for a further 10 minutes.

SERVES 10.

500 g (1 lb) haricot beans, soaked overnight
440 g (14 oz) canned tomatoes
3 tsp tomato purée
2 tbs oil
salt and pepper, to taste
1 tsp vinegar, malt or cider
1 tbs sugar

Green Beans with Flaked Almonds

Cook the beans in boiling water until tender. Melt half the butter or margarine in a frying pan. Add almonds and fry until golden brown, then remove from the pan. Melt the remaining butter or margarine and stir-fry the beans for 2-3 minutes. Add salt and pepper. Place in a serving dish and sprinkle with fried almonds.

Serve with mashed potato.

SERVES 4.

500 g (1 lb) French beans, quartered
60 g (2 oz) butter OR margarine
125 g (4 oz) almonds, flaked
salt and pepper, to taste

Broccoli with Ginger Sauce

Heat the oil and a little of the ginger in a wok or frying pan until hot. Stir-fry broccoli for 2-3 minutes or until tender. Combine soya sauce, stock or water, cornflour and the remaining ginger and pour over the broccoli, tossing and turning the broccoli until the sauce thickens.

SERVES 4-6.

1 tbs oil
1 tbs fresh ginger root, crushed
1 large broccoli, broken into small florets

SAUCE
2 tbs light soya sauce
125 ml (4 fl oz) vegetable stock OR water
2 tbs cornflour

Broccoli with Walnuts

Cook the broccoli in a saucepan with very little water and a tightly fitting lid until just tender. Heat the oil in a frying pan and fry the mushrooms for 2-3 minutes. Add walnuts, salt, pepper and mint. Continue frying until the walnuts are golden brown. Add the drained broccoli to the pan and cook over a high heat for 1 minute, stirring occasionally.

SERVES 4-5.

60 ml (2 oz) broccoli, broken into small florets
100 ml (3 fl oz) olive oil
60 g (2 oz) mushrooms, quartered
60 g (2 oz) walnuts, chopped
salt and pepper, to taste
1 tsp mint

Dhokra (Opposite)

For this recipe you will need a wok with a lid.

Mix all the batter ingredients (except the Eno) in a big bowl, adding enough warm water to make into a thick batter (like pancake batter). Divide the mixture into 3 equal portions. Quarter fill a wok with water and bring to the boil.

Meanwhile, add 1 teaspoon of Eno in each tray of batter and beat it thoroughly. Lightly oil a 20 x 25 cm (8 x 10 in) tray and pour the batter into the tray. Put the tray in the wok above the boiling water and cover immediately. Steam for 15 minutes, making sure that the wok does not boil dry.

Remove the tray from the wok (taking care not to get burnt in the steam). Allow to cool and cut into squares. Repeat with the remaining 2 portions of the batter.

For the topping, heat the oil in a saucepan. Add the sesame seeds and mustard seeds and cover with a lid. Once the seeds have popped, remove from the heat and spread with a spoon over each tray. Sprinkle with freshly chopped coriander leaves and chillies as desired and serve.

MAKES 3 TRAYS.

375 g (12 oz) gram flour (chick pea flour)
125 ml (4 oz) rice flour
250 ml (8 fl oz) plain yoghurt
1 tsp salt
2 tsp sugar
¼ tsp citric acid
3 tbs vegetable cooking oil
warm water
3 tsp Eno per tray

TOPPING
3 tbs cooking oil
2 tsp sesame seed (optional)
2 tbs desicated coconut
2 tsp mustard seeds
½ tsp chilli, finely chopped (optional)
1 tbs coriander leaves, freshly chopped

Brussels Sprouts au Gratin

Discard the outer leaves and wash the Brussels sprouts thoroughly. Steam for 5 to 7 minutes then place in a greased 25 x 30 cm (10 x 12 in) ovenproof dish. Cover with Cheese Sauce. Sprinkle the top with grated cheese and breadcrumbs.

Bake at 180°C/350°F/Gas Mark 4 for 20-25 minutes.

SERVES 6.

60 ml (2 oz) Brussels sprouts
Cheese Sauce (page 89)
30 g (1 oz) Cheddar cheese, grated
60 g (2 oz) breadcrumbs

Peperonata (Opposite)

Wash and dry the peppers and aubergine. Slice the peppers from top to bottom, remove the stem and slice into long fingers. Slice the aubergine from top to bottom, cut the slices in half widthways and then lengthways into fingers. Heat the oil in a frying pan or wok. Add the peppers and aubergine and cook on a high heat for 5 minutes. Add the chopped tomatoes and chilli. Cook for a further 5-8 minutes. Add salt and pepper to taste. Garnish with chopped parsley or coriander leaves.

Serve with Pitta Bread.

SERVES 4.

8 peppers (2 red, 2 orange, 2 yellow and
  2 green, or whatever is available)
1 aubergine (eggplant)
2 tbs olive oil OR sunflower oil
4 fresh tomatoes, chopped
1 fresh green chilli or red chilli, chopped
  (optional)
salt and pepper, to taste
parsley OR coriander leaves, chopped

Hungarian Courgettes

Melt half the butter or margarine, stir in the courgettes, cover and cook for 5-7 minutes. Melt the remaining butter or margarine and add the mushrooms, turning and cooking for 2-3 minutes. Mix all the ingredients, except the cheese, together in a large bowl. Transfer to an oven dish and bake at 160°C/325°F/Gas Mark 3 until crisp. Cover with the cheese and bake for a further 10 minutes.

SERVES 4.

125 ml (4 oz) butter OR margarine
500 g (1 lb) courgettes (zucchini), sliced
250 g (8 oz) mushrooms, sliced
440 g (14 oz) tomatoes, chopped
90 g (3 oz) fresh breadcrumbs
150 ml (¼ pint) sour cream
60 g (2 oz) almonds, flaked
1 tsp paprika
60 g (2 oz) Parmesan cheese, grated

Chick Pea and Coriander Patties

Drain and rinse the chick peas and blend them with oil in a food processor until smooth. Mix in the spices, coriander leaves and parsley. Stir in the flour, salt and pepper and leave for 15 minutes. Roll the mixture into 12 balls, the size of golf balls. Flatten into patties and fry in oil until golden.

Serve with Yoghurt (page 212) and Tomato Sauce (page 89).

MAKES 12 PATTIES.

500 g (1 lb) chick peas, soaked overnight
1 tbs oil
2 tsp cumin seeds, ground
2 tsp coriander seeds, ground
½ tsp chilli, ground (optional)
2 tsp coriander leaves, chopped
1 tbs parsley, chopped
2 tbs plain flour
salt and pepper, to taste
oil, for frying

Quick Pilau Rice (Opposite)

Wash the rice. Heat the oil in a pan, add mustard seeds, cumin seeds and asafoetida. Fry until the seeds pop. Add the frozen vegetables, salt and ginger and cook for 2 minutes. Add the water and stir in the rice. Cover the pan and cook on a low heat for about 20 minutes.

SERVES 3-4.

125 ml (4 oz) rice
2 tbs oil
¼ tsp mustard seeds
¼ tsp cumin seeds
pinch of asafoetida (hing)
60 g (2 oz) frozen mixed vegetables
1 tsp salt
1 tbs fresh ginger, crushed
450 ml (¾ pint) water
handful raisins

Jamaican Rice

Drain and rinse the red kidney beans. Pressure cook them until soft and drain them. Mix with rice, coconut cream, salt, mixed herbs or Jamaican thyme, asafoetida and chillies. Best served with salad.

Variation: If a pressure cooker is not available, cook the beans until tender. Substitute red kidney beans with adzuki beans or black eyed beans.

SERVES 4-6.

185 g (6 oz) red kidney beans (soaked for 1 hour
in hot water OR in cold water overnight)
500 ml (16 fl oz) water
250 g (8 oz) rice, cooked
60 ml (2 fl oz) coconut cream
salt, to taste
2 tsp mixed herbs OR Jamaican thyme
¼ tsp asafoetida (hing)
green chillies (optional)

Crunchy Cabbage

Discard the excess stalk and wash the cabbage thoroughly; then shred it. Bring the water and salt to the boil in a large saucepan and add the shredded cabbage. Cover and cook for 2-3 minutes. Drain well, place in a warm dish and keep hot.

Melt the butter or margarine in a saucepan, add peanuts, breadcrumbs and cheese and mix well. Spread over the cabbage and bake at 190°C/375°F/Gas Mark 5 for 10 minutes.

SERVES 4-5.

750 g (1½ lb) white cabbage
300 ml (½ pint) water
1 tsp salt
60 g (2 oz) butter OR margarine
60 g (2 oz) salted peanuts, chopped
30 g (1 oz) breadcrumbs
30 g (1 oz) mild Cheddar cheese, grated

Potato Pancakes (Opposite)

Wash, peel and coarsely grate the potatoes. Add salt, pepper and spices. Heat 1 tablespoon of butter, margarine or oil in a heavy-based frying pan. Add the potatoes, pressing evenly over the pan with a spoon. Cook, uncovered, over a medium heat for 8-10 minutes or until the underside is lightly browned. Turn the potato pancake over. You can add a little more butter, margarine or oil to the pan if required. Cook for further 8-10 minutes until the bottom is browned.

SERVES 7.

7 potatoes
½ tsp salt and pepper
1 tsp mixed spices
1 tbs butter OR margarine OR oil

Mushrooms and Tomatoes

Heat the oil in a pan and cook the tomatoes. Add the mushrooms and fry together. Add mint, salt and pepper. Cover and cook for 5-10 minutes.

Serve with croutons or toast.

SERVES 2.

2 tbs oil
2 large tomatoes, peeled and chopped
250 g (8 oz) mushrooms, sliced
1 tsp mint, chopped
salt and pepper, to taste

Fried Aubergine

Cut the aubergine into 1 cm (½ in) thick slices. Heat the butter or oil in a pan. Fry aubergine slices for about 1 minute each side, turning 3 or 4 times if necessary. Fry until crisp on the outside and tender inside. Turn onto a plate and sprinkle immediately with salt, pepper and basil.

SERVES 3.

1 large aubergine (eggplant)
2 tbs butter OR oil
salt and pepper, to taste
1 tsp basil

Roast Potatoes (Opposite)

In a saucepan, cover the potatoes with slightly salted boiling water, and boil until nearly cooked. Drain and place on a lightly greased baking tray. Sprinkle with dried rosemary or oregano, soya sauce, oil and peppercorns. Bake in a hot oven at 200°C/400°F/Gas Mark 6 for 1 hour until golden brown, turning occasionally.

SERVES 4-5.

500 g (1 lb) potatoes, peeled and quartered
boiling water, with a pinch of salt
1 tsp dried rosemary OR oregano
soya sauce, to taste
125 ml (4 fl oz) oil
a few crushed peppercorns

Lentil Rolls

Heat 3 tablespoons oil in a pan and gently fry celery, carrots and cabbage for 2-4 minutes. Add lentils, water and seasoning. Bring to the boil, cover and simmer for 50-60 minutes, stirring occasionally. Mix in the parsley and a third of the breadcrumbs. Leave to cool. Using floured hands, shape the mixture into cylindrical rolls and coat with the flour. Dip each roll into the milk and coat with the remaining breadcrumbs. Pour oil into a frying pan to a depth of 5 mm (¼ in) and place over a moderate heat. When hot, add the rolls and fry until crisp and golden brown, turning once or twice.

Serve with Yoghurt (page 212) and Cucumber Raita (page 40).

MAKES 10 ROLLS.

3 tbs oil
2 sticks celery, finely chopped
2 carrots, peeled and grated
60 g (2 oz) cabbage, finely shredded
280 g (9 oz) yellow lentils
600 ml (1 pint) water
salt and pepper, to taste
2 tbs fresh parsley, chopped
185 g (6 oz) wholemeal breadcrumbs
2 tbs flour
milk for coating
oil, for deep frying

Fried Rice

Put the rice into a saucepan or bowl. Wash and cook the mushrooms in a little boiling water until tender, then drain. The water can be reserved for soup or stock. Chop the mushrooms into small pieces, discarding the hard stems. Cut the tofu into small cubes and fry in a little oil until brown. Stir-fry the carrots separately in a little oil for 4-5 minutes and add to the rice. Put more oil in the wok and stir-fry the remaining vegetables for 3-4 minutes, adding soya sauce and pepper to taste. Mix all the vegetables lightly with the rice, finally adding the fried tofu. Sprinkle with sesame oil and serve.

SERVES 4-6.

500 g (1 lb) brown or white rice, cooked
125 ml (4 oz) dried Chinese mushrooms
125 ml (4 oz) firm tofu
3-4 tbs oil
2 carrots, diced
60 g (2 oz) sweetcorn, frozen
1 dried or fresh green pepper
1 dried or fresh red pepper
soya sauce
pepper
1 tbs sesame oil

Roast Parsnips

Cut the parsnips into 4 lengthways and place on a baking tray. Pour oil over the parsnips, sprinkle with salt and peppercorns and bake in hot oven at 200°C/400°F/Gas Mark 6 for 30 minutes or until golden-brown.

SERVES 4.

500 g (1 lb) parsnips, peeled
60 ml (2 fl oz) oil
pinch of salt
1 tbs peppercorns

Savoury Rice (Opposite)

Heat 2-3 tablespoons of oil in a wok and add ginger. Fry for 45 seconds, then add all the vegetables and stir-fry until tender. Add the cooked rice, salt, pepper, parsley or coriander and sesame oil and stir gently until mixed.

Serve hot.

SERVES 4-5.

3 tbs oil
30 g (1 oz) fresh ginger, crushed
60 g (2 oz) carrot, grated
60 g (2 oz) mushrooms, chopped
1 green pepper, chopped
60 g (2 oz) frozen corn
250 g (8 oz) rice (white or brown), already cooked
salt and pepper, to taste
a few fresh parsley OR coriander leaves
1 tsp sesame oil

Fried Rice Balls

Wash the rice and place in a saucepan with water and 1 teaspoon of salt. Bring to the boil, cover and simmer for 15 minutes or until tender.

Blend the flour with 2 teaspoons of salt, pepper and enough water to make a thick batter. In a separate bowl, blend milk, yoghurt and cornflour, and add to the rice. Add paprika or chillies, basil, cheese and mashed potato to the rice and mix until firm. Roll spoonfuls of mixture into walnut sized balls, dip into the batter until fully covered and fry in fairly hot oil until golden brown.

Serve hot with Tomato Sauce (page 89).

MAKES 10-12 BALLS.

250 g (8 oz) brown rice
600 ml (1 pint) water
3 tsp salt
280 g (9 oz) self-raising flour
1 tsp pepper
1 tbs milk
1 tbs yoghurt
1 tbs cornflour
1 tsp paprika OR 1-2 fresh chillies, chopped
handful of fresh basil, chopped
155 g (5 oz) Cheddar cheese, grated
2 medium-sized potatoes, cooked and mashed
oil, for deep frying

Savoury Vermicelli (Opposite)

Heat the oil in a large pan. Add cumin seeds and sauté for a few minutes. Then add all the vegetables. Stir in the salt, green chilli, ground turmeric, ground coriander and garam masala. When the vegetables are half cooked, add lemon juice to taste.

Half fill a medium sized pan with water and add 1 teaspoon of oil and ½ teaspoon of salt. Bring to the boil. Add the vermicelli and cook the vermicelli for 2-3 minutes. Drain out in a sieve.

Mix the vermicelli with the vegetables and let them cook for a few more minutes. Add fresh coriander leaves to garnish. Serve whilst hot.

SERVES 6.

2 tbs oil
½ tsp cumin seeds
2 potatoes, finely chopped
2 carrots, finely chopped
1 green pepper, finely chopped
60 g (2 oz) corn and 60 g (2 oz) peas OR
   125 ml (4 oz) mixed vegetables
3 fresh tomatoes, chopped
1 green chilli, chopped
½ tsp turmeric, ground
1 tsp coriander seeds, ground
1 tsp garam masala
lemon juice
1 tsp oil
½ tsp salt
250 g (8 oz) vermicelli
fresh coriander leaves, finely chopped

Green Beans and Tomato

Put all the ingredients into a saucepan. Bring to the boil, stirring constantly. Lower the heat and simmer for about 15 minutes until the beans are tender. Stir from time to time to prevent sticking.

Serve with bread or Pitta Bread.

SERVES 4-5.

500 g (1 lb) fresh or frozen runner beans, quartered
6 tbs tomato purée
4 tbs olive oil
250 ml (8 fl oz) water
salt and pepper, to taste
1 tsp oregano

Saffron Rice

Dissolve the saffron in hot water. Put the rice into a saucepan with cold water, salt and the saffron water. Bring to the boil, cover and simmer for 15 minutes or until tender. Sprinkle with almonds.

SERVES 3-4.

12 saffron threads, crushed slightly
2 tbs hot water
250 g (8 oz) white rice, washed
500 ml (16 fl oz) cold water
1 tsp salt
1 tbs almonds, flaked

Stuffed Mushrooms (Opposite)

Set the oven to 180°C/350°F/Gas Mark 4. Wash and remove the stalks from the mushrooms. Heat the oil in a frying pan, add the mushroom caps, rounded side down and fry for 1-2 minutes to soften. Place with rounded side down in an ovenproof dish. Chop the mushroom stalks and mix with parsley, cream, breadcrumbs and seasoning. Place a spoonful of this mixture in each mushroom cap. Melt the butter or margarine, stir in the flour, blend in the milk and add cheese when the sauce starts to thicken. Do not allow it to boil once the cheese is added. Spoon the sauce over the mushrooms and bake for 20 minutes until golden. Sprinkle with thyme and serve immediately.

SERVES 4.

6 large mushrooms
2 tbs oil
1 tbs fresh parsley, chopped
2 tbs cream
60 g (2 oz) breadcrumbs
salt and pepper, to taste
30 g (1 oz) butter OR margarine
30 g (1 oz) flour
300 ml (½ pint) milk
60 g (2 oz) mild Cheddar cheese, grated
½ tsp fresh thyme, chopped

Okra with Tomatoes

Wash okra and pat dry on kitchen paper; cut off the rounded caps at the stalk ends. Cut the peppers lengthways and remove the seeds. Chop the green pepper into pieces. Chop the red chilli pepper very finely. Heat the oil in a large saucepan and add the okra. Cook for 5-7 minutes over a medium heat. Add green pepper, chilli pepper, tomatoes, salt and pepper to the pan. Cover and simmer for a further 10 minutes, stirring occasionally, until the okra is tender. Sprinkle with chopped coriander leaves.

Serve with Yoghurt (page 212) and Cucumber Raita (page 40).

SERVES 4-5.

500 g (1 lb) small okra
1 small green pepper
1 small red chilli pepper
3 large tomatoes, chopped
3 tbs oil
salt and pepper, to taste
handful of coriander leaves, chopped

Paneer in Green Masala

Bring the milk to the boil, add the yoghurt and lemon juice. The milk should start to curdle and the paneer should separate from the water. Strain into a muslin cloth (or fine strainer), pat it flat, fold the muslin cloth over and place it under a heavy weight for 2-3 hours, to allow the water to drain out completely and for the paneer to set. When set, cut into 1 cm (½ in) cubes and keep aside. Paneer can be frozen.

Liquidise the tomatoes, coriander leaves, ginger and green chilli together. Add a little salt to retain the green colour.

In a frying pan, fry the cumin seeds and curry leaves in the oil until the seeds pop. Add the turmeric, garam masala and liquidised ingredients. Simmer for 15 minutes, then gently stir in the paneer and add salt to taste. Simmer for another 5 minutes.

Serve with rice or Chapatis (page 179).

SERVES 4.

PANEER
2.4 l (4 pints) full cream milk
150 ml (¼ pint) plain yoghurt
juice of 3 lemons

GRAVY
3-4 tomatoes
½ bunch of coriander leaves, finely chopped
  (about a cupful)
1 tbs ginger
1 green chilli (optional for an extra hot dish)
salt
1 tsp cumin seeds
8-10 curry leaves
1 tbs oil
½ tsp turmeric, ground
½ tsp garam masala

Pasta with Herbs

Fill a large saucepan ¾ full with water, bring to the boil, then add macaroni and cook until just tender. Drain well. Liquidise all the other ingredients, except the cucumber, in a blender for 2-3 minutes. Add to the pasta and mix in the cucumber.

Cool in the refrigerator before serving.

SERVES 3-4.

315 g (10 oz) pasta spirals
boiling water, with a pinch of salt and
  a few drops of oil
30 g (1 oz) fresh mixed herbs
2 tbs apple juice
1 tbs plain yoghurt
¼ tsp mustard
60 ml (2 fl oz) buttermilk
2 tbs olive oil
salt and pepper, to taste
1 cucumber, finely sliced

Potato Balls

Boil and mash the potatoes. Heat 2 tablespoons of oil in a saucepan, add the mustard seeds and wait until they pop. Add the ginger and chillies and fry them for a couple of seconds. Mix this into the mashed potato and add salt, lemon juice and fresh coriander. Form the mixture into small balls about 2.5 cm (1 in) in diameter. For the batter, mix the flour, salt, oil and water into a thick smooth batter. Dip the potato balls into the batter and deep-fry them until golden.

Serve hot with Tomato Sauce (page 89).

MAKES 20-25 BALLS.

BALLS
1 kg (2 lb) potatoes
oil, for frying
½ tsp mustard seeds
1 tbs ginger, crushed
2 fresh green chillies, seeded and chopped
1 level tsp salt, to taste
juice of ½ lemon
1 tbs fresh coriander, chopped

BATTER
185 g (6 oz) gram flour (chick pea flour)
1 level tsp salt
1 tbs of oil
150 ml (¼ pint) water
oil, for deep frying

Desserts

Apple Crunch
Baked Apples
Baked Bananas
Apple Pie
Banana Pudding
Christmas Pudding
Custard
Date Sauce
Fried Pineapple
Fruit Cream Delight
Fruit Cream Dessert
Fruit Crumble
Fruit Juice Jelly
Fruit Salad—Fresh
Fruit Salad—Grated
Fruit Shortbread
Halva
Ice Cream
Ice Cream—Chocolate
Ice Cream—Chocolate with
    Almonds
Jam Tart
Lemon Flan
Mince Pies
Mince Tart
Peach Sorbet
Stuffed Apples
Strawberry Tarts
Sweet Vermicelli
Tapioca Pudding
Trifle
Yoghurt Ice
Yoghurt Orange Whip

Apple Crunch

Peel and slice the apples and put them into a pan with 3-4 tablespoons sugar and the water. Cook until soft. Break the bread into pieces and grind into crumbs. Melt the butter or margarine in a saucepan, add the breadcrumbs and demerara sugar and fry gently over a low heat until golden brown. Leave to cool. Arrange layers of breadcrumb mixture and apples in a glass dish, finishing with a layer of breadcrumbs. Chill in the refrigerator. Whip the cream and spread on top of the crumbs. Sprinkle grated chocolate over the cream.

SERVES 4-6.

500 g (1 lb) cooking apples
2 tbs water, to cover
3-4 tbs sugar
125 g (4 oz) brown bread
60 g (2 oz) butter OR margarine
60 g (2 oz) demerara sugar
150 ml (¼ pint) whipping cream
60 g (2 oz) plain chocolate, grated

Baked Apples (Opposite)

Set the oven to 190°C/375°F/Gas Mark 5. Wash the apples and remove the cores using an apple corer. Place the apples on a baking tray and fill the centres with sugar, raisins or sultanas and golden syrup. Bake for 20-30 minutes until cooked.

Serve with Custard (page 119).

SERVES 4.

4 cooking apples
3 tbs brown sugar
90 g (3 oz) raisins OR sultanas
3 tbs golden syrup

Baked Bananas

Slice each banana in half lengthwise and then again across the width. Place in an ovenproof dish and cover with butter or margarine, sugar and lemon juice. Bake in the oven at 200°C/400°F/Gas Mark 6 for 15 minutes, basting once or twice.

Serve with whipped cream.

SERVES 3.

500 g (1 lb) ripe bananas
60 g (2 oz) butter OR margarine
60 g (2 oz) sugar
2 tbs lemon juice
300 ml (½ pint) whipped cream

Apple Pie

Prepare the pastry by sifting the flour and salt, and rubbing in the butter or margarine until the mixture resembles fine breadcrumbs. Add sufficient cold water to make a firm dough. Roll out thinly and evenly. Line a 25 cm (10 in) flan dish with pastry. Line the flan pastry with greaseproof paper or aluminium foil and fill with dried beans. Bake blind in a hot oven at 200°C/400°F/Gas Mark 6 for 10 minutes. Remove the beans and paper or foil. Keep the beans to use again.

Fill the pastry crust with apple pulp, which should not be too moist. Sprinkle with cinnamon and sultanas.

Mix oats, butter or margarine and sugar together and spread over the top. Alternatively, make lattice strips from leftover pastry and sprinkle with sugar. Bake at 180°C/350°F/Gas Mark 4 for 30 minutes.

Serve with cream.

SERVES 8-10.

BASE
315 g (10 oz) flour, wholemeal or plain
pinch of salt
125 g (4 oz) butter OR margarine
cold water, to mix
dried beans, for baking blind

FILLING
440 g (14 oz) apples, cooked and pulped
1 tsp cinnamon, ground
2 tbs sultanas

TOPPING
125 g (4 oz) oats
60 g (2 oz) butter OR margarine
1 tbs muscovado sugar

Banana Pudding

Peel bananas and slice 1 cm (½ in) thick. Arrange in a 20 x 25 cm (8 x 10 in) baking dish. Mix coconut, sugar, cardamom and cashews together and spread over the sliced bananas. Pour the coconut milk over the top. Bake at 150°C/300°F/Gas Mark 2 until the moisture is absorbed and the bananas are cooked. Garnish with pistachios.

Serve with double cream.

SERVES 4-6.

4-6 large bananas
125 g (4 oz) desiccated coconut
60 g (2 oz) brown sugar
¼ tsp cardamom, ground
1 tbs cashew nuts, ground
500 ml (16 fl oz) coconut milk
1 tbs pistachio nuts, chopped
300 ml (½ pint) double cream

Christmas Pudding

Mix the flour, baking powder and breadcrumbs together. In a separate bowl, mix the remaining ingredients thoroughly. Stir in the flour and breadcrumb mixture. Transfer the pudding mixture to a greased bowl, leaving 5 cm (2 in) at the top to allow for rising. Cover with foil, secured with a rubber band, and steam for 6-8 hours. The pudding may be kept for a week or two. It should be steamed for an hour before using.

Serve with Custard or Date Sauce (see below).

SERVES 6-8.

60 g (2 oz) 100% wholemeal flour
½ tsp baking powder
125 g (4 oz) 100% wholemeal breadcrumbs
90 g (3 oz) sultanas
90 g (3 oz) currants
185 g (6 oz) seeded raisins
1 tsp orange peel, grated
2 tbs lemon juice
½ tsp mixed spice
125 ml (4 fl oz) soya milk
100 ml (3 fl oz) vegetable oil
1 tbs molasses

Custard

Mix the custard powder in a bowl with 2 tablespoons of cold milk. Heat up the milk. When it is warm, remove from the heat. Add the sugar and stir. Add the custard powder and whisk vigorously to remove any lumps. Return the custard to the heat and bring to the boil. Remove from the heat and add the nutmeg and/or vanilla essence.

MAKES 1 PINT OF CUSTARD.

600 ml (1 pint) cold milk
2 ½ tbs custard powder
2 tbs sugar
1 pinch of nutmeg and/or a few
  drops of vanilla essence

Date Sauce

Liquidise dates in soya milk. Discard coarse pieces. Mix the cornflour into a smooth paste with 4 tablespoons of soya milk. Heat the date mixture to boiling point, then add the cornflour paste, stirring vigorously. Sweeten to taste with brown sugar and flavour with vanilla.

SERVE ON CHRISTMAS PUDDING.

125 g (4 oz) dates
600 ml (1 pint) soya milk
125 g (4 oz) cornflour
4 tbs brown sugar
1 tsp vanilla essence

Fried Pineapple

Peel and cut the pineapple into small chunks. Place the butter or margarine and sugar in a frying pan over a low heat until the sugar has dissolved. Add pineapple chunks and cook for a further 15 minutes, stirring occasionally until the pineapple chunks are coated. Add orange juice and coconut, stir and leave to cool. Whip the double cream until it thickens.

Serve the coated pineapple chunks with cream.

SERVES 5-6.

500 g (1 lb) fresh pineapple
30-60 g (1-2 oz) butter OR margarine
90 g (3 oz) light brown sugar
3 tbs orange juice
2-3 tbs desiccated coconut
250 ml (8 fl oz) double cream

Fruit Cream Delight

Blend most of the strawberries, sugar, grape juice and half of the cream. Place half the jam in 6 small dessert bowls, cover with half the apricots and then half the blended mixture. Repeat the layers, finishing with cream. Refrigerate. Just before serving, decorate with 1 or 2 fresh strawberries.

SERVES 6.

470 g (15 oz) strawberries
2 tsp sugar
1 tbs black grape juice
250 ml (8 fl oz) whipped cream
155 g (5 oz) Strawberry Jam (page 210)
155 g (5 oz) fresh apricots, chopped

Fruit Cream Dessert

Chop the fruit into small cubes. Mix sour cream and yoghurt in a separate bowl and add vanilla, nutmeg and sugar according to taste. Add fruit and mix. Serve chilled.

SERVES 4.

500 g (1 lb) fresh fruit of your choice
150 ml (¼ pint) sour cream
150 ml (¼ pint) plain yoghurt
1 tsp vanilla essence
pinch of nutmeg, ground
125 g (4 oz) brown sugar

Fruit Crumble

Set the oven to 180°C/350°F/Gas Mark 4. Sprinkle the fruit with half the sugar. Mix and place in a 25 cm (10 in) baking dish. Prepare the crumble by mixing flour and remaining sugar in a mixing bowl, rubbing in butter or margarine until the mixture resembles breadcrumbs, and adding oats. Sprinkle the crumble mixture over the fruit. Bake for 20-30 minutes or until light golden brown. Top with demerara sugar.

Serve with fresh cream or Custard (page 119).

SERVES 4-6.

500 g (1 lb) fresh fruit, finely chopped
  —citrus fruit is unsuitable
125 g (4 oz) sugar, for fruit
125 g (4 oz) plain flour
1 tbs mixed spice (optional)
60 g (2 oz) butter OR margarine
60 g (2 oz) rolled oats
1 tbs demerara sugar

Fruit Juice Jelly

Blend the agar agar to a smooth paste with a little of the water. Add the remaining water and the fruit juice, transfer to a pan and bring to the boil. Cook for 2-3 minutes. Remove from the heat and pour into a mould. When cool put in the refrigerator and leave to set.

SERVES 2-4.

3 tsp agar agar
300 ml (½ pint) water
300 ml (½ pint) fruit juice

Fruit Salad—Fresh

Halve the grapes and dice all the fruit. Soak the raisins in apple or orange juice for 1 hour. Mix all these ingredients together. Add sugar and sprinkle with coconut. Add more juice if necessary.

Serve with fresh cream, Yoghurt (page 212) or Custard (page 119).

SERVES 6.

125 g (4 oz) seedless grapes
2 kiwi fruits
2 bananas
4 peaches
2 ripe pears
125 g (4 oz) raisins
600 ml (1 pint) apple OR orange juice
sugar, to taste
1 tbs coconut

Fruit Salad—Grated

Grate pears and apples and sprinkle with lemon juice. Place in small dessert bowls and drizzle with honey. Sprinkle with nuts and cinnamon.

Quantities of honey, nuts and cinnamon can be varied according to taste. Use a combination of almonds, hazelnuts and walnuts.

SERVES 4-5.

2 conference pears
2 eating apples
juice of ½ lemon
2 tbs honey
60 g (2 oz) mixed nuts, ground
1 tsp cinnamon, ground

Fruit Shortbread

Set the oven to 180°C/350°F/Gas Mark 4. Mix the flours and sugar and rub in the butter or margarine until the mixture resembles breadcrumbs. Press the mixture into a 28 cm (11 in) baking tray. Bake for 20 minutes until golden brown.

Cover the base with jam. Spread drained pineapple over the jam. Sprinkle sugar over the fruit and bake in the oven until cooked.

Serve with fresh cream.

SERVES 5-6.

185 g (6 oz) flour
1 tbs rice flour
60 g (2 oz) icing sugar
60 g (2 oz) butter OR margarine

FILLING
250-315 g (8-10 oz) Apricot Jam (page 210)
440 g (14 oz) canned pineapple, small chunks
60 g (2 oz) sugar

Halva (Opposite)

Melt the butter or margarine in a fairly large saucepan over a low heat. Add in the semolina and stir continually until golden brown. Reduce the heat and then gently pour in the hot water or milk, stirring all the time until the mixture becomes like smooth paste, taking care not to burn it. Add sugar, almonds, cardamom and raisins. Mix everything together, reduce heat and cook for a further 2-3 minutes.

Serve hot.

SERVES 6-7.

250 g (8 oz) butter OR margarine
90 g (3 oz) coarse semolina
1.5 l (2½ pints) hot water OR milk
220 g (7 oz) sugar
60 g (2 oz) almonds, chopped
pinch of cardamom, ground
60 g (2 oz) raisins

Ice Cream

Place the can of evaporated milk in a freezer for a few hours. Remove it and let it defrost. Cream it with an electric mixer until light and fluffy. Add the double cream and vanilla essence and whisk until thick. Add the sugar and mix well. Pour it into a plastic container and decorate with nuts and glacé cherries. Place the container in the freezer to set.

Vanilla essence can be replaced by any flavour of your choice.

SERVES 4.

300 ml (½ pint) canned unsweetened
   evaporated milk
600 ml (1 pint) double cream
1½ tsp vanilla essence
10–12 tbs caster sugar
mixed nuts, chopped for decoration (optional)
glacé cherries for decoration (optional)

Ice Cream–Chocolate

Heat the milk and sugar together, without letting them boil. Whisk the cream until it is quite thick. Add milk, sugar and chocolate to the cream, stir and put into a plastic container. When it is frozen (about 1–2 hours) whisk again. Return to the freezer until frozen solid.

150 ml (¼ pint) milk
60 g (2 oz) caster sugar
300 ml (½ pint) double cream
60 g (2 oz) chocolate, melted

Ice Cream–Chocolate with Almonds

Mix together single cream, double cream and condensed milk. Stir well. Put the cocoa powder into a small bowl and slowly add enough boiling water to make a thick paste. Add the mixture to the cream and milk. Stir well and add vanilla or almond essence. Place the mixture into the freezer for 1-2 hours, then into an ice-cream machine, following the directions for your machine. You may add roasted almonds to the mixture as it freezes.

300 ml (½ pint) single cream
300 ml (½ pint) double cream
375 ml (12 oz) sweetened condensed milk
1½-2 tsp cocoa powder
boiling water, to mix
1 tsp vanilla or almond essence
roasted almonds, chopped (optional)

Jam Tart

Combine flour, salt and sugar. Rub in the oil or margarine and then mix in the water to create a soft dough. Roll it out to 1 cm (½ in) thick. Oil and flour a round baking tray. Line the tray with the pastry and trim off the excess pastry. Spread the jam on top evenly with a knife. Decorate with pastry strips.

Bake at 190°C/375°F/Gas Mark 5 for approximately 20 minutes, until the pastry is cooked.

Serve with cream or Custard (page 119).

SERVES 4-6.

250 g (8 oz) self-raising flour
pinch of salt
125 g (4 oz) sugar
30 g (1 oz) oil OR margarine
water, to mix
jam, for the filling (page 206–210)

Lemon Flan

Melt the butter or margarine. Crush the biscuits into crumbs and mix with the butter or margarine. Press the mixture into a lightly greased 20 x 25 cm (8 x 10 in) flan case. Whip together cream, condensed milk and lemon juice. Spoon into the flan case and chill.

SERVES 4-6.

125 g (4 oz) butter OR margarine
250 g (8 oz) ginger nut biscuits
150 ml (¼ pint) double cream
440 g (14 oz) sweetened condensed milk
1–2 tbs lemon juice to taste

Mince Pies

Sift the flour, add the sugar and rub the butter or margarine and fat into the flour. Add the water to form a dough. As the pastry is extra rich, it is important to allow it to become firm in the refrigerator for at least 30 minutes. Roll the pastry out onto a floured board and cut into 24 rounds. Put into greased cupcake trays, fill with mincemeat and cover with pastry lids.

Bake at 400°F/200°C/Gas Mark 6 for 25 minutes. Allow to cool, then dredge the tops with icing sugar.

MAKES 24 MINCE PIES.

500 g (1 lb) plain flour
60 g (2 oz) caster sugar
250 g (½ lb) butter OR margarine
90 g (3 oz) vegetable fat
2 tbs water
Mincemeat (page 205)
icing sugar, to dust

Mince Tart

Sift the flour, rub in the fat and add water to make a soft dough. Refrigerate for half an hour. Roll out on a floured board to cover a 20 or 23 cm (8 or 9 in) pie dish. Fill generously with Mincemeat. Lay strips of pastry over the mincemeat to make a lattice and bake at 200°C/400°F/Gas Mark 6 for about 30 minutes.

Serve with Custard (page 119).

SERVES 4-6.

PASTRY
250 g (8 oz) self-raising flour
125 g (4 oz) vegetable fat
3-4 tbs cold water to bind
410 g (13 oz) Mincemeat (page 205)

Peach Sorbet

Boil the water and sugar in a small saucepan and stir until the sugar has dissolved. Remove from the heat and leave to cool. Purée the peaches in a blender. Mix the syrup and peach purée together. Add lemon juice to taste. Pour into a freezing tray or plastic container and leave in the ice-making compartment of a refrigerator for 1½ hours, or until frozen 2.5 cm (1 in) at the sides. Scrape into a chilled bowl and whisk until smooth. Return to the tray and freeze for at least 1 hour, or until firm.

SERVES 6-8.

150 ml (¼ pint) water
45 g (1½ oz) granulated sugar
500 g (1 lb) canned peaches
2-2½ tsp lemon juice

Stuffed Apples

Set the oven to 180°C/350°F/Gas Mark 4. Wash and core the apples using an apple corer. Mix the sugar, dates and nuts together. Place the cored apples on a greased baking tray and stuff with the nut and date mixture. Bake for 45-50 minutes.

Serve hot or cold.

SERVES 4.

4 large cooking apples
60 g (2 oz) sugar
90 g (3 oz) dates, chopped
60 g (2 oz) mixed nuts, chopped

Strawberry Tarts

Sift flour and salt into a mixing bowl. Cut the butter or margarine and rub into the flour until the mixture looks like breadcrumbs. Gradually add water until a firm dough is formed. Keep the dough in the refrigerator for 30–45 minutes before rolling it out. Roll out the pastry to 5 mm (¼ in) thick. Cut out rounds with a tumbler or pastry cutter and transfer to a greased patty tin. Prick the base of each tart with a fork.

Bake at 200°C/400°F/Gas Mark 6 for 12 minutes or until light golden brown in a hot oven. Leave to cool. Whip the double cream with the vanilla essence. Fill each tart with one or two strawberries and a teaspoonful of whipped cream, then sprinkle with caster sugar.

MAKES 30 TARTS.

125 g (4 oz) plain flour
½ tsp salt
60 g (2 oz) butter OR margarine
cold water, to mix
450 ml (¾ pint) double cream
¼ tsp vanilla essence
500 g (1 lb) fresh strawberries
caster sugar, for sprinkling

Sweet Vermicelli

Melt the butter or margarine in a saucepan, add in the vermicelli and fry until golden brown. Pour in the milk and cook the vermicelli for 30 minutes or until soft. Stir gently to prevent it from sticking at the bottom. Add in the sugar, cardamom and nuts. Simmer until the milk thickens slightly.

SERVES 6-8.

60 g (2 oz) butter OR margarine
125 g (4 oz) vermicelli
900 ml (1½ pints) milk
185 g (6 oz) sugar
½ tsp cardamom, ground
60 g (2 oz) almonds, chopped
60 g (2 oz) pistachios, chopped

Tapioca Pudding

Wash the tapioca in cold water. Bring the milk to the boil, add the tapioca and stir continually until it is cooked. Add sugar and almonds to taste.

SERVES 4.

60 g (2 oz) tapioca (small or large grains)
600 ml (1 pint) milk
30–60 g (1–2 oz) almonds, chopped
sugar, to taste

Trifle (Opposite)

Cover the base of a bowl with pieces of sponge cake. Spread the fruit evenly over the sponge cake. Prepare the jelly, pour it onto the fruit and leave it to set in the refrigerator for 1 hour. Meanwhile, prepare the custard and allow it to cool. Completely cover the jelly and cake with custard. Whip the double cream and spread it evenly over the custard. Sprinkle with grated chocolate and leave in the refrigerator for 1 hour before serving.

SERVES 8-10.

Plain Sponge Cake (page 134)
60 g (2 oz) seedless grapes
185 g (6 oz) canned peaches
185 g (6 oz) canned pineapple
600 ml (1 pint) Fruit Juice Jelly (page 121)
600 ml (1 pint) Custard (page 119)
300 ml (½ pint) double cream
60 g (2 oz) cooking chocolate, grated

Yoghurt Ice

Keep a few strawberries for decoration. Place all the ingredients in a blender and liquidise, then pour into small deep dishes. Freeze for 3-4 hours in the freezer. Decorate with strawberries before serving.

SERVES 4-6.

500 g (1 lb) fresh strawberries
300 ml (½ pint) natural yoghurt
2 tbs golden syrup
250 ml (8 fl oz) double cream

Yoghurt Orange Whip

Peel the oranges and save the peel. Chop the flesh and blend with honey and yoghurt in the blender. Chill and top with nuts and grated orange rind.

SERVES 4.

8 oranges
2 tbs honey
600 ml (1 pint) yoghurt
nuts, chopped for topping

Cakes,
Biscuits and Decorations

Apple Cake
Simple Chocolate Cake
Plain Sponge Cake
Chocolate Sponge Sandwich
Chocolate Sponge Sandwich
    with Fruit
Christmas Cake
Carrot Cake
Chocolate Sponge Cake
Date Cake
Fruit Cake
Walnut Cake
Cheesecake
Fruit Loaf
Chocolate Burfi
Sugarless Cake
Little Sesame Cakes
Quick Cherry Loaf
Orange and Coconut Cake
Easy Cake
Tea Cakes
Almond Biscuits
Banana Flapjacks
Chocolate Biscuits

Chocolate Chip Cookies
Chocolate Cookies
Chocolate Date Bars
Cocoa Biscuits
Custard Powder Biscuits
Flapjacks
Finger Biscuits
Coconut Biscuits
Ginger Biscuits
Nutty Date Sweet
Hazelnut Squares
Oat Biscuits
Oat Cakes
Oatmeal Cookies
Orange Shortcake Biscuits
Pecan Puffs
Quick Peanut Butter Cookies
Sesame Snaps
Shortbread
Star Biscuits
Butter Cream
Chocolate Curls and Leaves
Chocolate Icing
Grated Chocolate

Apple Cake

Peel the apples and remove the cores. Chop roughly into slices and put into a pan with 2 tablespoons of water. Cover and stew until soft.

Meanwhile, cream the fat and sugar together in a bowl large enough to hold the whole of the cake mixture. Sift the flour into a separate bowl with the mixed spice, baking powder, walnuts and raisins or other dried cake fruit. By now, the apples should be cooked and cooled. Transfer the cooked apples into the bowl and mix thoroughly with a wooden spoon.

Set the oven temperature to midway between 160°C/325°F/Gas Mark 3 and 180°C/350°F/Gas Mark 4. Lightly grease two 25 cm (10 in) cake tins and line them with paper. Blend the flour with the apple mixture. Mix thoroughly and turn at once into the tins. Decorate with almonds, if desired. Place the cake tins just above the centre of the oven, and bake for about 1¼ hours. Leave to cool before turning out.

Non-stick tins should be greased lightly. Other tins should be lined with greaseproof paper or a silicon-treated baking parchment.

MAKES 2 CAKES.

1 kg (2 lb) cooking apples
2 tbs water
155 g (5 oz) soft white vegetable fat
375 g (12 oz) brown sugar
750 g (1½ lb) self-raising flour
2 tsp mixed spice
2 tsp baking powder
60 g (2 oz) walnuts, chopped
375 g (12 oz) raisins OR other dried cake fruit
almonds, flaked, for decoration (optional)

Simple Chocolate Cake (Opposite)

Set the oven to 200°C/400°F/Gas Mark 6. Melt the butter or margarine for 2 minutes in the microwave and pour into a large mixing bowl. Add condensed milk, vanilla essence and half the milk and beat together. Add the cocoa and the sponge flour or plain flour and baking powder slowly, using a spatula to fold in the mixture with the other half of the milk. The texture should be smooth and of dropping consistency. Cover a 20-25 cm (8-10 in) baking tin with greaseproof paper and spread the mixture evenly 2 cm (1 in) deep equally over the tin. Bake for 10-15 minutes or until golden brown. When it comes out of the oven, place another tray over it, turn it over and peel off the greaseproof paper. When the cake has cooled, cover with cling film to keep it moist.

The top can be iced with Chocolate Icing (page 158).
For a coffee and chocolate flavoured cake, add 2 teaspoons of diluted coffee.

155 g (5 oz) butter OR margarine
440 g (14 oz) sweetened condensed milk
1 tsp vanilla essence
250 ml (8 fl oz) milk
4 tbs cocoa powder
315 g (10 oz) sponge flour OR
315 g (10 oz) plain flour and
  ½ tsp baking powder

Plain Sponge Cake

Sift the flour, custard powder, salt, baking powder and bicarbonate of soda into a bowl. Whisk the milk, oil, yoghurt, syrup and vanilla essence together in another bowl. Add the caster sugar and whisk further.

Add this to the dry ingredients and mix well to form a smooth mixture. Pour this mixture into a greased 23 cm (9 in) cake tin and bake in a hot oven at 180°C/350°F/Gas Mark 4 for about 40-50 minutes.

Variation: add 3 tbs cocoa powder with the flour.

375 g (12 oz) sponge flour OR self-raising flour
2 tbs custard powder
½ tsp salt
½ tsp baking powder
1 tsp bicarbonate of soda
450 ml (¾ pint) milk
180 ml (6 fl oz) oil
1 tsp vanilla essence
2 tbs plain yoghurt
3 tbs golden syrup
280 g (9 oz) caster sugar

Chocolate Sponge Sandwich

Sift flour, cocoa, sugar and bicarbonate of soda into a bowl. Put the butter or margarine, syrup, and milk and water into a small saucepan and cook over a very gentle heat until the butter or margarine has melted. When just tepid, pour onto the dry ingredients and mix to a smooth batter with a wooden spoon. Turn into a 20 x 5 cm (8 x 2 in) greased sandwich tin, and bake at 200°C/400°F/Gas Mark 6 for 30 minutes. Cool on a rack and, when cold, cut in half and spread with Chocolate Icing. The top can also be iced or simply sprinkled with icing sugar.

FOR A STEAMED CHOCOLATE SPONGE SANDWICH
This is a useful alternative if an oven is not available. Turn the mixture into a greased cake tin 13 cm (5 in) in diameter and cover with greased paper. Place in a steamer, cover with a tightly fitting lid and steam gently over boiling water for 1 hour. Remove the paper cover and leave to stand for a few minutes before turning out. Cool on a wire rack.

155 g (5 oz) self-raising flour
30 g (1 oz) cocoa
30 g (1 oz) sugar
½ tsp bicarbonate of soda
60 g (2 oz) butter OR margarine
1 tbs golden syrup
6 tbs milk and water, mixed
Chocolate Icing (page 158) OR
 icing sugar, for sprinkling

Chocolate Sponge Sandwich with Fruit

Prepare the cake mixture as for Chocolate Sponge Sandwich. Divide it equally between two 21 cm (8½ in) diameter sandwich tins. Bake as for Chocolate Sponge Sandwich. While the cakes are in the oven, prepare the filling.

Whip the cream until stiff. Sift the icing sugar into the cream, and add the fruit. Mix well. Allow the cakes to cool in their tins until completely cold, then turn out one cake onto a plate or cake board. Spread the whipped cream filling over it. Place the second cake on top to complete the chocolate sponge sandwich. Dust with icing sugar.

155 g (5 oz) self-raising flour
30 g (1 oz) cocoa
30 g (1 oz) sugar
½ tsp bicarbonate of soda
60 g (2 oz) butter OR margarine
1 tbs golden syrup
6 tbs milk and water, mixed
Chocolate Icing (page 158) OR
  icing sugar, for sprinkling

FILLING
150 ml (¼ pint) double or whipping cream
1 tbs icing sugar
125 g (4 oz) strawberries OR 125 g (4 oz) raspberries
  OR 1 peeled mango, finely cubed
icing sugar, for decoration

Christmas Cake

Mix the molasses, lemon juice, orange rind, oil, soya milk and fruit together thoroughly. Sift the flour, baking powder and mixed spice together and stir into the fruit mixture. Turn into a 20 cm (8 in) non-stick cake tin.

Bake at 150°C/300°F/Gas Mark 2 for 2 hours. Cover with greaseproof paper, and bake at 120°C/250°F/Gas Mark ½ for another hour or until a skewer inserted into the cake comes out clean and dry. Decorate with nuts, if desired, or cover with marzipan after baking.

1 tbs molasses
1 tbs lemon juice
1 tsp orange rind, grated
125 ml (4 fl oz) vegetable oil
300 ml (½ pint) soya milk
250 g (8 oz) currants
250 g (8 oz) sultanas
125 g (4 oz) seeded raisins
375 g (12 oz) wholemeal flour
1 tsp baking powder
1 tsp mixed spice
chopped nuts and marzipan for decoration (optional)

Carrot Cake

Set the oven to 190°C/375°F/Gas Mark 5. Mix the sugar, oil, vinegar, milk and vanilla in a large bowl. Sift flours, salt, bicarbonate of soda, cinnamon and baking powder into the mixture. Add the carrots, pecans or walnuts and pineapple and mix well. Transfer to a greased 20 cm (8 in) cake tin. Bake in the oven for 30-35 minutes. Allow to cool before removing from the tin.

Beat the butter, cream cheese, vanilla, icing sugar and nuts together well and spread them evenly over the cooled cake.

Any variety of nuts can be used for decoration.

125 g (4 oz) sugar
125 ml (4 fl oz) vegetable oil
4 tsp malt vinegar
180 ml (6 fl oz) milk
1 tsp vanilla essence
125 g (4 oz) white self-raising flour
125 g (4 oz) wholemeal self-raising flour
1 tsp salt
2 tsp bicarbonate of soda
2 tsp cinnamon
2 tsp baking powder
375 g (12 oz) carrot, grated
125 g (4 oz) pecan OR walnuts, chopped
125 g (4 oz) pineapple, crushed (no juice)

FROSTING
125 g (4 oz) butter
250 g (8 oz) cream cheese
1 tsp vanilla essence
250 g (8 oz) icing sugar
125 g (4 oz) nuts, chopped

Chocolate Sponge Cake

Put the chocolate, butter or margarine and milk into a saucepan and melt over a low heat (it should not boil). Mix well and leave to cool a little. Sift the flour, salt and bicarbonate of soda together in a bowl. Stir in the sugar. Add the vanilla to the chocolate and gradually mix the melted ingredients into the dry ingredients. Spoon into a greased and paper lined, round 20 cm (8 in) cake tin.

Bake at 180°C/350°F/Gas Mark 4 for 20 minutes. Leave to cool before turning out.

60 g (2 oz) plain chocolate
90 g (3 oz) butter OR margarine
250 ml (8 fl oz) milk
220 g (7 oz) self-raising flour
pinch of salt
¾ tsp bicarbonate of soda
125 g (4 oz) sugar
1 tsp vanilla essence

Date Cake

Put the dates and water into a small saucepan, bring slowly to the boil, simmer very gently for 5 minutes and then leave to cool. Sift the flour, mixed spice, sugar and bicarbonate of soda into a bowl and rub in the butter or margarine. Pour the date mixture into the flour and mix thoroughly with a wooden spoon. Turn into a greased shallow tin 20 x 5 cm (8 x 2 in), spread smoothly with a wet knife and bake at 190°C/375°F/Gas Mark 5 for 40 minutes. Leave to cool before turning out.

125 g (4 oz) dates, chopped
60 ml (2 fl oz) water
155 g (5 oz) self-raising flour
¼ tsp mixed spice
60 g (2 oz) sugar
1 tsp bicarbonate of soda
60 g (2 oz) butter OR margarine

Fruit Cake

Rub the butter or margarine into the flour. Add the sugar, currants, sultanas, candied peel and milk and mix thoroughly. Dissolve the bicarbonate of soda in water and add to the mixture. Then add the vinegar. Turn into a 18 cm (7 in) diameter cake tin lined with greaseproof paper and bake at 190°C/375°F/Gas Mark 5 for 1½ hours. Leave to cool before turning out.

125 g (4 oz) butter OR margarine
250 g (8 oz) plain flour
90 g (3 oz) soft brown sugar
90 g (3 oz) currants
125 g (4 oz) sultanas
30 g (1 oz) candied peel
150 ml (¼ pint) milk
1 tbs bicarbonate of soda
1 tbs tepid water
1 tbs malt or balsamic vinegar

Walnut Cake

Melt the butter or margarine and beat in the sugar and evaporated milk. Add the flour, baking powder, salt and vanilla essence and gradually mix in the nuts and the milk. Transfer to a greased 25 cm (10 in) baking tin and bake at 180°C/350°F/Gas Mark 4 for 35-40 minutes. Leave to cool before removing from the tin.

90 g (3oz) chopped walnuts
125 g (4 oz) butter OR margarine
280 g (9 oz) sugar
125 ml (4 fl oz) evaporated milk
590 g (19 oz) plain flour
¾ tsp baking powder
pinch of salt
1 tsp vanilla essence
180 ml (6 fl oz) milk

Cheesecake (Opposite)

Mix the flour, mixed nuts, butter and sugar together and press into a greased and lined 20 cm (8 in) tin. Bake at 180°C/350°F/Gas Mark 4 for 20 minutes. Allow to cool before adding cheesecake mix.

Mix together cream cheese, lemon peel, grated lemon juice, sugar, vanilla essence, yoghurt and milk. Pour on top of the base and bake at 160°C/325°F/Gas Mark 3 for 25 minutes. Cool for 5 minutes.

Mix together sour cream, sugar and vanilla, pour over the cheesecake and bake at 160°C/325°F/Gas Mark 3 for 7 minutes. Leave to cool in the refrigerator for a minimum of 2 hours before serving.

The Cheesecake can be decorated with pistachios, fruit or fruit jam.

BASE
185 g (6 oz) plain flour
60 g (2 oz) mixed nuts, (walnuts, cashews and almonds) finely chopped
60 g (2 oz) butter, melted
2 tbs sugar

FILLING
500 g (1 lb) cream cheese
2 tsp lemon peel, grated
1½ tbs lemon juice
90 g (3 oz) sugar
1½ tsp vanilla essence
2 tbs plain yoghurt
5 tbs milk

TOPPING
500 ml (16 oz) sour cream
45 g (1½ oz) sugar
2 tsp vanilla essence

Fruit Loaf

Mix the bran, sugar and fruit well together in a bowl. Stir in the milk and leave to stand for half an hour. Sift in the flour, mixing well, and pour into a well greased 1 kg (2 lb) loaf tin.

Bake at 180°C/350°F/Gas Mark 4 for 1 hour. Leave to cool before turning out of the tin. Cut into slices.

125 g (4 oz) bran
155 g (5 oz) caster sugar
315 g (10 oz) mixed dried fruit
300 ml (½ pint) milk
125 g (4 oz) self-raising flour

Chocolate Burfi (Opposite)

Melt the butter in a saucepan, add the milk and coconut and cook over a low heat. Add the milk powder, sugar, almonds and cardamom, stirring continuously until all the ingredients are mixed together. Grease a baking sheet and a rolling pin with butter. Put the mixture onto the baking sheet and spread it evenly with the rolling pin. Allow the burfi to cool. Melt the chocolate over hot water and spread it evenly over the burfi. Allow the chocolate to set before cutting in small squares. Keep in the refrigerator until serving.

60 g (2 oz) butter
250 ml (8 fl oz) milk
155 g (5 oz) coconut
250 g (8 oz) milk powder
185 g (6 oz) sugar
90 g (3 oz) almonds, ground
pinch of cardamom seeds, ground
250 g (8 oz) cooking chocolate
butter, for greasing

Sugarless Cake

Heat the dates and water gently in a saucepan until soft, then mash the dates into rough pieces. Add the dried fruit, flour, baking powder, mixed spice, grated rind and orange juice. Mix well and spoon into a 1 kg (2 lb) loaf tin lined with greaseproof paper. Level the top and sprinkle with almonds.

Bake at 160°C/325°F/Gas Mark 3 for 1½ hours, or until a skewer inserted into the cake comes out clean and dry. If the top of the cake is becoming too brown before the end of cooking time, cover it with greaseproof paper. Cool a little before turning out of the tin.

250 g (8 oz) cooking dates, chopped
300 ml (½ pint) water
500 g (1 lb) mixed dried fruit
185 g (6 oz) plain wholewheat flour
3 tsp baking powder
1 tsp mixed spice
rind of 1 orange OR lemon, grated
4 tbs orange juice
almonds, halved or chopped

Little Sesame Cakes

Heat the milk, water, oil and sugar gently in a saucepan until the sugar dissolves. Set aside to cool. Sift the flour with bicarbonate of soda, cinnamon and mixed spice or nutmeg into a bowl. Add the sesame seeds and currants. Set the oven at 180°C/350°F/Gas Mark 4. Add the liquid to the flour mixture and stir well. Put about 1 tablespoon of the mixture into each baking case. Bake for about 20 minutes.

MAKES 48 SESAME CAKES.

300 ml (½ pint) milk
500 ml (16 fl oz) water
300 ml (½ pint) oil
500 g (1 lb) brown sugar
750 g (1½ lb) wholemeal flour
2 tsp bicarbonate of soda
2 tsp cinnamon, ground
1 tsp mixed spice OR nutmeg, ground
185 g (6 oz) sesame seeds
375 g (12 oz) currants

Filling:
50g (2 oz) sultanas
1 lemon, juice only
225g (8 oz) golden syrup
100g (4 oz) fresh white breadcrumbs
1. Heat oven to 180°C, 350°F, Gas No. 4. Have ready an 18cm (7 inch) pie plate.
2. Place the flour, salt and lemon rind in a bowl. Rub in the margarine until the mixture resembles breadcrumbs. Stir in enough cold water to bind the mixture to a dough.
3. Knead lightly on a floured surface, roll out the pastry and use to line the pie plate. Trim the edges and flute.
4. Place the sultanas in a saucepan with lemon juice and simmer gently until all the juice has been absorbed. Add the golden syrup and heat until melted then stir in the breadcrumbs. Pour into the pastry case and spread level.
5. Bake for about 40 minutes until filling is beginning to
For best results use either metric OR imperial

Quick Cherry Loaf (Opposite)

Set the oven to 180°C/350°F/Gas Mark 4. Prepare a 500 g (1lb) loaf tin by lightly greasing it and lining the base with greaseproof paper. Place all the ingredients, except the decoration and glaze, in a bowl and mix well. Pour the mixture into the tin. Smooth out the top. Decorate with cherries and walnuts. Bake for 1 hour. Allow to cool, then turn out. Brush with honey and serve in slices spread with butter or margarine.

250 ml (8 fl oz) milk
125 g (4 oz) glacé cherries, halved
125 g (4 oz) soft brown sugar
250 g (8 oz) self-raising flour
1 tsp mixed spice
cherries and walnuts, halved for decoration
honey, to glaze

Orange and Coconut Cake

Mix the flour, baking powder, most of the coconut, butter or margarine, sugar, most of the orange rind, yoghurt, milk and cornflour in a bowl and mix well for 2–3 minutes, until a thick batter is formed. Grease two 18 cm (7 in) sandwich tins and line the base with greaseproof paper. Put the mixture into the tins and bake at 180°C/350°F/Gas Mark 4 for 30–35 minutes. Leave to go cold.

Mix the icing sugar and orange juice or water together. Sandwich the 2 cakes together with a thin layer of the icing and spread the rest on top. Sprinkle with the remaining coconut and orange rind.

250 g (8 oz) self-raising flour
3 tsp baking powder
60 g (2 oz) desiccated coconut
250 g (8 oz) softened butter OR margarine
250 g (8 oz) sugar
rind of 2 oranges, grated
4 tbs plain yoghurt
4 tbs milk
4 tbs cornflour
125 g (4 oz) icing sugar
1–2 tbs orange juice OR water

Easy Cake (Opposite)

Mix the oil, orange juice and vanilla essence together in a mixing bowl. Stir in the flour and sugar. Mix well and pour into a greased, shallow 20 cm (8 in) cake tin and bake at 200°C/400°F/Gas Mark 6 for 30-35 minutes. Leave to cool before removing from the tin.

250 ml (8 fl oz) cooking oil
250 ml (8 fl oz) fresh orange juice
½ tsp vanilla essence
410 g (13 oz) sponge flour OR
 self-raising flour
125 g (4 oz) caster sugar

Tea Cakes

Mix the butter or margarine, sugar, nutmeg, colouring, custard powder, baking powder and vanilla together to a smooth, fluffy mixture. Add milk and mix. Gradually add flour, sultanas and coconut. Mix thoroughly and put tablespoons of the mixture into paper baking cases.

Bake at 190°C/375°F/Gas Mark 5 for 20-25 minutes. Decorate with almonds or walnuts.

MAKES 50 TEA CAKES.

500 g (1 lb) butter OR margarine
625 g (1¼ lb) caster sugar
pinch of nutmeg, ground
1 tsp yellow food colouring
1½ tsp custard powder
1½ tsp baking powder
½ tsp vanilla essence
600 ml (1 pint) milk
1.125 kg (2¼ lb) self-raising flour
125 g (4 oz) sultanas
125 g (4 oz) coconut
almonds OR walnuts, chopped for decoration

Almond Biscuits

Mix the butter or margarine, sugar, vanilla essence or nutmeg, milk and bicarbonate of soda until creamy. Add the almonds and flour and roll into small balls.

Bake on a greased baking tray at 180°C/350°F/Gas Mark 4 for 15-20 minutes.

MAKES 50 BISCUITS.

500 g (1 lb) butter OR margarine
315 g (10 oz) sugar
1 tsp vanilla essence OR pinch of nutmeg, ground
125 ml (4 fl oz) milk
1 tsp bicarbonate of soda
500 g (1 lb) almonds, ground
1 kg (2 lb) plain flour, sifted

Banana Flapjacks

Grease an 18 x 28 cm (7 x 11 in) Swiss roll tin. Set the oven to 180°C/350°F/Gas Mark 4. Cream the butter or margarine until soft, then beat in the sugar, honey and banana. Stir in the flour and oats. Spoon into the Swiss roll tin and spread evenly. Bake towards the top of the oven for 25-30 minutes. Cut into fingers in the tin while still warm. Then leave to become quite cold before removing from the tin and separating the fingers.

MAKES 16-18 FLAPJACKS.

90 g (3 oz) butter OR margarine
125 g (4 oz) demerara sugar
1 tbs honey
1 banana, peeled and mashed
60 g (2 oz) plain flour
250 g (8 oz) rolled oats

Chocolate Biscuits

Beat the butter or margarine, almond essence and sugar until creamy. Sift in the flour and form into a smooth paste. Spoon the mixture into a piping bag fitted with a large star nozzle. Pipe rounds onto 2 greased baking trays.

Bake at 160°C/325°F/Gas Mark 3 for 10-12 minutes or until pale golden. Cool on baking trays until firm, then transfer to a wire rack and leave to cool.

Break the chocolate into a bowl and leave to melt over a pan of simmering water. Dip half of each biscuit into the chocolate. Leave the biscuits in a cool place until the chocolate has set.

MAKES 12 BISCUITS.

250 g (8 oz) softened butter OR margarine
¼ tsp almond essence
125 g (4 oz) caster sugar
250 g (8 oz) plain flour, sifted
125 g (4 oz) chocolate

Chocolate Chip Cookies

Beat the butter or margarine and sugar until creamy. Add all other ingredients, except milk, and mix well. Add sufficient milk to bind the mixture. Form into balls and place well apart on a greased tray.

Bake at 180°C/350°F/Gas Mark 4 for 10 minutes or until lightly browned.

The balls of dough can be frozen and baked when required.

MAKES 34-36 COOKIES.

125 g (4 oz) butter OR margarine
250 g (8 oz) brown sugar
1 tsp baking powder
75 g (2½ oz) coconut, shredded
75 g (2½ oz) rolled oats
60 g (2 oz) self-raising flour
125 g (4 oz) milk or white chocolate chips
2 tsp vanilla essence
125 g (4 oz) plain flour
milk, to mix

Chocolate Cookies

Mix the flour, almonds and salt together in a bowl. Rub in the butter or margarine. Divide into 2 parts. Add chocolate to 1 part. Work each part into a soft dough with milk and vanilla. Chill both the doughs for 1 hour and knead lightly, one dough at a time, on a floured board. Roll out separately to a rectangle 5 mm (¼ in) thick. Place the rectangle of chocolate dough on top of the plain dough and trim the edges so that they are the same size. Starting at the long edge, very carefully roll the chocolate and plain doughs up together so that they form a long sausage. Chill for 30 minutes to make it easier to cut. With a sharp knife, cut into 1 cm (½ in) thick slices. Place flat on a greased baking tray.

Bake at 190°C/375°F/Gas Mark 5 for 20-25 minutes or until firm.

MAKES 15 COOKIES.

315 g (10 oz) plain flour, sifted
60 g (2 oz) almonds, ground
pinch of salt
185 g (6 oz) butter OR margarine
90 g (3 oz) plain chocolate, melted
milk, to mix
1 tsp vanilla essence

Chocolate Date Bars

Put the water, flour, dates, chocolate and vanilla in a small saucepan and cook for 10 minutes on low heat. Leave to cool. In a bowl, mix together the flour, oats and sugar and rub in the butter or margarine. Spread half the crumble mixture over the base of a 25 x 30 cm (10 x 12 in) baking tin, pressing it down firmly. Cover with filling, then the remainder of the crumble. Press down with a rounded knife.

Bake at 190°C/375°F/Gas Mark 5 in the centre of the oven for about 25 minutes or until golden brown. Allow it to cool for 10 minutes, then turn out onto a board or other flat surface. Cut into fingers.

MAKES 12 FINGERS.

FILLING
150 ml (¼ pint) water
2 tsp flour
185 g (6 oz) dates
125 g (4 oz) chocolate
¼ tsp vanilla essence

CRUMBLE
125 g (4 oz) self-raising flour
155 g (5 oz) rolled oats
125 g (4 oz) light soft brown sugar
185 g (6 oz) butter OR margarine

Cocoa Biscuits

Mix the butter or margarine, sugar, bicarbonate of soda, milk and vanilla or nutmeg. Add the flour and form into a soft dough. Divide the dough into 2 equal parts. Add cocoa powder to 1 part, kneading it until the cocoa powder is merged into the dough. Roll out each dough separately, less than 5 mm (¼ in) thick. Place one on top of the other and roll them over together into a log shape. Cut the roll into slices, 1 cm (½ in) thick and place on a greased baking tray.

Bake at 180°C/350°F/Gas Mark 4 for 20-30 minutes.

MAKES 25-30 BISCUITS.

500 g (1 lb) butter OR margarine
500 g (1 lb) sugar
1 tsp bicarbonate of soda
1 tbs milk
1 tsp vanilla essence OR nutmeg, ground
1.25 kg (2½ lb) plain flour
3 tbs cocoa powder

Custard Powder Biscuits

Sift all the dry ingredients together. Rub in the butter or margarine. Knead very well without adding any liquid. Form into small balls. Press on each ball with the back of a fork, crosswise.

Bake them on a greased baking tray at 200°C/400°F/Gas Mark 6 for about 12 minutes.

MAKES 18-20 BISCUITS.

185 g (6 oz) plain flour
60 g (2 oz) custard powder
60 g (2 oz) icing sugar, sifted
2 tsp baking powder
pinch of salt
155 g (5 oz) butter OR margarine

Flapjacks

Melt the sugar, butter or margarine and syrup. Add oats and salt, mixing all the time. Press the mixture into a flat greased 25 x 28 (10 x 11 in) baking tray and bake at 180°C/350°F/Gas Mark 4 for 20 minutes. When cool, cut into squares.

MAKES 12-16 FLAPJACKS.

250 g (8 oz) soft brown sugar
250 g (8 oz) butter OR margarine
4 tsp golden syrup
500 g (1 lb) rolled oats
pinch of salt

Finger Biscuits

Set the oven to 180°C/350°F/Gas Mark 4. Put the butter or margarine, sugar and syrup into a pan and heat gently until the butter has melted. Stir in the cinnamon, almonds, raisins, sesame seeds and oats and mix well. Roll out the pastry to 5 mm (¼ in) thick and line the bottom of a 25 x 28 cm (10 x 11 in) baking tray with it. Press the oats mixture down on top of the pastry using the back of a spoon.

To decorate, evenly space the glacé cherries on the top and bake in a hot oven at 180°C/350°F/Gas Mark 4 for 25-30 minutes. Whilst still warm, cut into slices. Allow to cool completely before removing from the tray.

MAKES 8-10 FINGER BISCUITS.

125 g (4 oz) butter OR margarine
125 g (4 oz) soft brown sugar
3 tbs golden syrup
1 tsp cinnamon, ground
60 g (2 oz) almonds, flaked
60 g (2 oz) raisins
60 g (2 oz) sesame seeds
90 g (3 oz) rolled oats
125 g (4 oz) puff pastry
6 glacé cherries, halved

Coconut Biscuits (Opposite)

Mix the butter or margarine, sugar, baking powder, custard powder and essence in a bowl. Add milk and mix until smooth. Add flour, coconut and semolina and form into a soft dough. Roll into small balls and place on a greased baking tray.

Bake at 180°C/350°F/Gas Mark 4 for 20-25 minutes.

MAKES 25-30 BISCUITS.

250 g (8 oz) butter OR margarine
60 g (2 oz) sugar
2 tsp baking powder
3 tsp custard powder
½ tsp rose essence
125 ml (4 fl oz) milk
60 g (2 oz) plain flour
500 g (1 lb) desiccated coconut
60 g (2 oz) semolina

Ginger Biscuits

Set the oven to 190°C/375°F/Gas Mark 5. Mix the butter or margarine, sugar, golden syrup, ginger, baking powder, bicarbonate of soda and warm milk until soft and smooth. Add the flour and semolina and form a soft dough. Roll out to 5 mm (¼ in) thick and cut with a biscuit cutter. Prick each biscuit with a fork and place on a greased baking tray. Bake for 15 minutes.

MAKES 25-30 BISCUITS.

125 g (4 oz) butter OR margarine
125 g (4 oz) sugar
250 g (8 oz) golden syrup
1½ tbs ginger powder
1½ tsp baking powder
1 tsp bicarbonate of soda
1 tbs warm milk
500 g (1 lb) plain flour
1 tbs semolina

Nutty Date Sweet (Opposite)

Melt the butter or margarine in a saucepan, add dates and cook over low heat until they begin to soften. Add nutmeg or cardamom and nuts. Mix thoroughly until all nuts are blended into the date mixture. Put the mixture on an oiled surface, oil the palms of your hands and make two thick rolls. Place the rolls on a tray and refrigerate for 24 hours. Put the rolls on a chopping board and slice into 6 mm (¼ inch) thick rounds. Store in a tin.

MAKES 25-30 PIECES.

60 g (2 oz) butter OR margarine
500 g (1 lb) dried stoned dates, chopped
pinch of nutmeg OR cardamom, ground
90 g (3 oz) almonds, chopped
90 g (3 oz) pistachios, chopped
90 g (3 oz) cashews, chopped

Hazelnut Squares

Cream the butter or margarine and the sugar. Stir in the flours and ground hazelnuts. Mix lightly. Spread the dough evenly into a 25 x 30 cm (10 x 12 in) tin. Mark into squares and place a whole hazelnut on each square.

Bake at 150°C/300°F/Gas Mark 2 for 30-40 minutes until golden brown.

MAKES 16-18 SQUARES.

250 g (8 oz) butter OR margarine
60 g (2 oz) caster sugar
185 g (6 oz) plain flour
45 g (1½ oz) rice flour
125 g (4 oz) hazelnuts, ground
16-18 whole hazelnuts, roasted
water to mix

Oat Biscuits

Mix butter or margarine, sugar, bicarbonate of soda and honey or golden syrup until the mixture becomes fluffy. Then add flour, coconut and oats and mix well to form the dough. Take small amounts of the dough, shape them into rounds, put on a greased baking tray and prick them with a fork.

Bake at 180°C/350°F/Gas Mark 4 for 20-25 minutes.

MAKES 30-35 BISCUITS.

500 g (1 lb) butter OR margarine
250 g (8 oz) sugar
1 tsp bicarbonate of soda
2 tbs honey OR golden syrup
625 g (1¼ lb) plain flour
250 g (8 oz) desiccated coconut
250 g (8 oz) rolled oats
water to mix

Oat Cakes

Mix oats, salt and baking powder. Rub in the butter or margarine. Add water to form a dry dough. Form into balls, flatten and place on a greased baking tray. Prick with a fork.

Bake at 200°C/400°F/Gas Mark 6 for 20-25 minutes.

MAKES 25 OAT CAKES.

750 g (1½ lb) oats
1 tsp salt
2 tsp baking powder
155 g (5 oz) butter OR margarine
water, to mix

Oatmeal Cookies

Mix the apple juice, salt and oil in a bowl. Stir in the oats and walnuts. Add enough flour to make a stiff dough. Form the dough into small balls and shape into cookies on a greased baking tray.

Bake at 190°C/375°F/Gas Mark 5 until golden brown.

MAKES 25 COOKIES.

75 ml (2½ fl oz) apple juice
½ tsp salt
4 tbs oil
500 g (1 lb) rolled oats
60 g (2 oz) walnuts, chopped
flour, to mix

Orange Shortcake Biscuits

Melt the butter or margarine. Mix all the dry ingredients in a large mixing bowl with the melted butter or margarine. Add the orange rind and the orange juice, and mix. Roll out the mixture to a thickness of 8 cm (3 in) and place in the refrigerator for 2 hours. Cut it into 5 mm (¼ in) square slices and place on a greased baking tray.

Bake at 180°C/350°F/Gas Mark 4 for 15-20 minutes.

220 g (7 oz) butter OR margarine
360 g (11½ oz) plain flour
220 g (7 oz) sugar
1 tsp baking powder
½ tsp bicarbonate of soda
1 tsp orange rind, grated
60 ml (2 fl oz) orange juice

Pecan Puffs

Cream the sugar and butter or margarine together. Add vanilla essence and nuts. Slowly sift in the flour. Roll into 2 cm (¾ in) balls and bake them on a greased baking tray at 160°C/325°F/Gas Mark 3 for 30 minutes. Whilst still hot, roll them in icing sugar.

MAKES 30 PUFFS.

60 g (2 oz) sugar
250 g (8 oz) butter OR margarine
2 tsp vanilla essence
155 g (5 oz) pecan nuts, ground
90 g (3 oz) pecan nuts, chopped
280 g (9 oz) wholemeal flour
icing sugar, for rolling
water to mix

Quick Peanut Butter Cookies

Combine all the ingredients in a large bowl and mix well. Drop a tablespoon of batter onto a greased baking tray for each cookie. Bake at 180°C/350°F/Gas Mark 4 for 10-12 minutes or until golden brown.

MAKES 16-18 COOKIES.

125 g (4 oz) peanut butter
60 g (2 oz) raisins
125 g (4 oz) self-raising flour
440 g (14 oz) sweetened condensed milk
1 tsp lemon juice
60 ml (2 fl oz) milk

Sesame Snaps

Melt the butter or margarine slowly over a low heat. Add the sugar and honey, stirring all the time with a wooden spoon. Add the sesame seeds and keep stirring to blend evenly. Add coconut and porridge stirring continuously. Press the mixture into a greased Swiss roll tin 33 x 23 cm (13 x 9 in).

Bake at 150°C/300°F/Gas Mark 2 for 30 minutes. Cut into squares when cool.

MAKES 24 SNAPS.

185 g (6 oz) butter OR margarine
90 g (3 oz) sugar
100 ml (3 fl oz) honey
60 g (2 oz) sesame seeds
140 g (4½ oz) desiccated coconut
185 g (6 oz) porridge oats

Shortbread

Set the oven to 160°C/325°F/Gas Mark 3. Sift the flours together and add the butter or margarine and sugar. Rub together with your fingertips until the mixture begins to bind. Press the mixture into a 25 x 28 (10 x 11 in) greased baking tray. Prick the top of the mixture with a fork and bake for 35 minutes or until golden brown. Remove from the oven and allow to cool before cutting. Sprinkle caster sugar on top of the shortbread.

MAKES 16-20 SLICES.

250 g (8 oz) plain flour
125 g (4 oz) rice flour
250 g (8 oz) butter OR margarine
125 g (4 oz) sugar
caster sugar, for sprinkling

Star Biscuits (Opposite)

Set the oven to 180°C/350°F/Gas Mark 4. Sift the icing sugar into a bowl, add butter or margarine, cut into pieces, and cream together until light and fluffy. Sift in the flours and add water to make a smooth dough. Leave in the refrigerator to harden for 1 hour.

Place on a floured surface. Form into small balls, and flatten with your palm. Cut into star shapes using a star cutter. Place the stars on a greased baking tray and bake for 15-20 minutes.

Decorate with coloured icing and hundreds-and-thousands.

MAKES 24 BISCUITS.

250 g (8 oz) butter OR margarine
90 g (3 oz) icing sugar
250 g (8 oz) plain flour
125 g (4 oz) cornflour
2-4 tbs water

Butter Cream

Cream the butter until soft and gradually beat in the sugar, adding the milk and a few drops of vanilla essence.

125 g (4 oz) butter
185 g (6 oz) icing sugar
1–2 tbs milk
a few drops of vanilla essence

Chocolate Curls and Leaves (Opposite)

Chocolate curls are made with a vegetable peeler or knife on the flat base of a bar of chocolate. Chocolate leaves are made by painting one side of clean, deep veined rose leaves with melted chocolate. Cool on waxed paper. Turn the chocolate leaves over, so that the chocolate side is on the palm of your hand, and peel the leaf away carefully.

Chocolate

Chocolate Icing

Cream the butter until soft and gradually beat in the sugar, adding the milk and cocoa or drinking chocolate powder.

125 g (4 oz) butter
185 g (6 oz) icing sugar
1–2 tbs milk
2 tbs cocoa OR drinking chocolate powder

Grated Chocolate

Grate large pieces of chocolate, finely or coarsely, in a rotary hand grater, food processor or hand-held grater. Rinse hands in cold water to prevent stickiness.

Chocolate

Treats

Almond Crunch
Banana Crunch
Chocolate Rice Crisps
Bliss Balls
Chocolate Nuts and Dried Fruit
Chocolate Spread
Chocolate Truffles
Coconut Ice
Coconut Pyramids
Coconut Squares
Coffee and Chocolate Truffles
Easy Fudge
Gulab Jamun
Nut Crunch
Date Fingers
Peppermint Cream
Ice Lollies
Toffee
Toffee Apples

Almond Crunch

Dissolve the sugar in a pan over a low heat, add water and bring to the boil. Lower heat and add saffron, almonds and butter or margarine, stirring all the time. When the mixture thickens, pour into a greased dish, spread evenly and sprinkle the top with cardamom. Cut into squares.

MAKES 6-8 PIECES.

125 g (4 oz) sugar
5 tbs water
pinch of saffron
125 g (4 oz) almonds, ground
125 g (4 oz) unsalted butter OR margarine
pinch of cardamom, ground

Banana Crunch

Put banana in a small bowl, cover with yoghurt and sprinkle with sugar, sultanas and wheat flakes.

SERVES 2.

1 banana, sliced
300 ml (½ pint) plain yoghurt
1 tbs sugar
30-60 g (1-2 oz) sultanas
30 g (1 oz) wheat flakes

Chocolate Rice Crisps (Opposite)

Break the chocolate into a large bowl and melt by placing over boiling water or putting in the microwave for 2 minutes. Mix in the Rice Crispies until thoroughly coated with chocolate. Whilst still warm, spoon the mixture into paper baking cases. Leave to cool.

Alternative: use cornflakes instead of Rice Crispies, but the cornflakes should be slightly crushed.

MAKES 50 CRISPS.

500 g (1 lb) cooking chocolate
345 g (11 oz) Rice Crispies

Bliss Balls

Melt the butter or margarine and mix with sugar and milk. Add dry ingredients and vanilla essence, mix well, roll into balls and dip in the coconut. Place in refrigerator to set.

MAKES 12-14 BALLS.

125 g (4 oz) butter OR margarine
6 tbs sugar
5 tbs milk
12 tbs milk powder
3 tbs cocoa powder OR drinking chocolate
125 g (4 oz) sultanas
½ tsp vanilla essence
desiccated coconut, for coating

Chocolate Nuts and Dried Fruit

Melt the chocolate in a bowl over hot water. Dip the dried fruit and nuts into the chocolate, one piece at a time, and place on an oiled baking tray. Put the tray in the refrigerator to harden the chocolate. Store in a tin.

MAKES NEARLY 100 PIECES.

500 g (1 lb) cooking chocolate, plain or milk
60 g (2 oz) dried mango slices
60 g (2 oz) dried apricots
60 g (2 oz) large currants
60 g (2 oz) large sultanas
60 g (2 oz) whole almonds, blanched
60 g (2 oz) Brazil nuts
60 g (2 oz) hazelnuts

Chocolate Spread

Place all the ingredients in a saucepan over a low heat. Stir continuously until everything is melted and blended. Leave to cool before transferring to a jar and storing.

2 tbs cocoa powder
125 g (4 oz) butter OR margarine
125 g (4 oz) golden syrup

Chocolate Truffles

With a rolling pin, crush the biscuits to a fine powder and put into a bowl. Add syrup and water. Melt the butter or margarine and chocolate. Add to biscuits and beat well. Stir in the almond essence. Divide mixture into small balls and roll them in the chocolate vermicelli.

MAKES 6-8 TRUFFLES.

125 g (4 oz) sweet biscuits
1 tbs golden syrup
1 tbs hot water
30 g (1 oz) butter OR margarine
60 g (2 oz) chocolate, melted
1 tsp almond essence
chocolate vermicelli (chocolate sprinkles), for coating

Coconut Ice

Mix the coconut, condensed milk and vanilla essence with a spoon to make a stiff dough. Add more coconut if the mixture is very moist. Grease a baking sheet and spread the mixture evenly on it. Leave in refrigerator for 2-3 hours or until it hardens. When the coconut is hard, sprinkle icing sugar on and cut into pieces.

MAKES 18-20 ICES.

250 g (8 oz) desiccated coconut
400 g (13 oz) sweetened condensed milk
1 tsp vanilla essence
315 g (10 oz) icing sugar

Coconut Pyramids

Set the oven to 160°C/325°F/Gas Mark 3. Combine all the ingredients. Divide the mixture into 13 little balls and shape into cones. Bake for 10 minutes.

MAKES 13 PYRAMIDS.

250 g (8 oz) desiccated coconut
1 tsp vanilla essence
5 tbs condensed milk

Coconut Squares (Opposite)

Mix water and sugar in a saucepan and bring to the boil. Reduce heat and simmer until it becomes a light thin syrup. Add desiccated coconut. Sprinkle in the milk powder, cardamom and food colouring, whilst continuing to stir over a low heat. Remove from the heat, place on a greased tray and roll out to 6 mm (¼ inch) thick. Decorate with nuts. When cool, cut into squares. Keeps for 10 days.

MAKES 10-12 SQUARES.

1.5l (2½ pints) water
90 g (3 oz) sugar
250 g (8 oz) fine desiccated coconut
45 g (1½ oz) milk powder
pinch of cardamom, ground
3-4 drops food colouring (optional)
almonds and pistachios, chopped for decoration

Coffee and Chocolate Truffles

Mix coffee and water and allow to cool. Put syrup, cocoa, butter or margarine and cream into a pan. At first, stir over a low heat until well mixed and then bring to the boil. Remove from the heat, add coffee liquid and stir in the sugar. Beat until smooth and allow to cool. Roll the mixture into balls. Roll each ball in the cocoa, place in an airtight tin and store in the refrigerator.

MAKES 20 TRUFFLES.

4 tbs black coffee
1 tbs hot water
1½ tbs golden syrup
60 g (2 oz) cocoa
60 g (2 oz) butter OR margarine
2 tbs double cream
155 g (5 oz) icing sugar
cocoa, for coating

Easy Fudge

In a saucepan, heat together butter or margarine and water. Stir together until melted and then bring to the boil. Sift together sugar, milk powder and cocoa powder. If the mixture seems lumpy, then sift again. Add the butter or margarine and stir until well combined. Add nuts and turn onto a greased baking tin 20 x 20 x 5 cm (8 x 8 x 2 in). Cover and chill for several hours or till firm. Cut into squares.

MAKES 750 G (1½ LB) OF FUDGE.

60 g (2 oz) butter OR margarine
80 ml (2½ fl oz) water
500 g (1 lb) icing sugar
60 g (2 oz) non fat dry milk powder
60 g (2 oz) unsweetened cocoa powder
60 g (2 oz) nuts, chopped

Gulab Jamun (Opposite)

Mix all the ingredients for the syrup in a large pan and bring to the boil. Lower the heat and simmer for 30 minutes. The syrup is now ready.

Put aside to cool to room temperature.

Add the ground cardamom and saffron to the milk and bring to the boil. Take the pan off the heat and stir in the evaporated milk.

Mix the milk powder, plain flour, bicarbonate of soda and 3 teaspoons of oil in a large bowl. Slowly add the milk mixture and knead into a soft smooth dough.

Make small smooth balls (either round or oval shaped) about 18 mm (¾ inch) in diameter.

Heat the oil mixed with 3 tablespoons of ghee and fry the Jamuns, about 20 at a time, on an extremely low heat until they rise.

Once risen and expanded, turn to a high heat and fry until golden or dark brown.

Drain the Jamuns on a kitchen towel and leave aside for 2 minutes.

Add the Jamuns to the cooled syrup and soak for 2-3 hours before serving.

MAKES 40 GULAB JAMUNS.

SYRUP
500 g (1 lb) sugar
500 ml (16 fl oz) water
½ tsp cardamom, freshly ground
a few strands of saffron

JAMUNS
¼ tsp cardamom seeds, freshly ground
a few strands of saffron
125 ml (4 fl oz) milk
220 ml (7 fl oz) evaporated milk
300 ml (½ pint) milk powder
105 g (3½ oz) plain flour
½ level tsp bicarbonate of soda
3 tbs ghee (clarified butter)
oil, for deep frying

Nut Crunch

Moisten the rolling pin with oil. Place sugar, oil and lemon juice in a pan and stir over a high heat. Stir continuously and within 10 minutes the sugar will turn to a smooth light brown liquid. As soon as this happens, remove from the heat immediately. Very quickly add the nuts or whatever you have chosen. If necessary add more nuts until you reach the desired consistency. All this must be done very quickly. Place on an oiled board and roll flat. Let it cool for 10 minutes then cut into squares.

To store: place cellophane paper between the layers to avoid sticking and store in an airtight container. Keeps for one month.

MAKES 25 PIECES.

45 g (1½ oz) sugar
1 tbs oil
2 drops of lemon juice
155 g (5 oz) chopped nuts
  OR sesame seeds
  OR dried sliced coconut
  OR roasted chick peas

Date Fingers

Combine flour and muesli. Rub in the butter or margarine and fold in the sugar. Combine the dates, lemon juice and water in a saucepan and cook over a low heat until soft. Press half the crumble mixture into a greased 18 cm (7 in) square baking tin. Spread with the date mixture and press the remaining crumble mixture on top.

Bake at 180°C/350°F/Gas Mark 4 for 30 minutes.

MAKES 25 FINGERS.

CRUMBLE
125 g (4 oz) self-raising flour
125 g (4 oz) muesli
125 g (4 oz) butter OR margarine
60 g (2 oz) brown sugar

FILLING
250 g (8 oz) dates, chopped
2 tbs lemon juice
3 tbs water

Peppermint Cream

Mix icing sugar to a stiff paste with top of the milk. Add peppermint essence. Knead until quite smooth, adding more icing sugar or milk, if necessary, to make a paste which can be rolled out. Roll out to 6 mm (¼ inch) thick and cut into rounds or whatever shapes you desire. Place on greaseproof paper to set.

250 g (8 oz) icing sugar
2 tbs top of the milk
½ tsp peppermint essence

Ice Lollies

Mix the ingredients in a jug and pour into ice-cube or ice-lolly moulds. Leave in the freezer until solid.

MAKES 6 LOLLIES.

250 ml (8 fl oz) orange squash
1-2 tsp lemon juice, undiluted
1 tsp caster sugar

Toffee (Opposite)

Melt the butter or margarine and sugar in a saucepan. Add condensed milk and syrup. Allow to boil slowly for 20 minutes, stirring all the time. Toffee can be tested by dropping a little in water—if it hardens, it is ready. Before removing from the heat, add vanilla essence. Pour the mixture on a well-greased tray and spread evenly.

90 g (3 oz) butter OR margarine
155 g (5 oz) sugar
400 g (13 oz) sweetened condensed milk
1 tbs golden syrup
¼ tsp vanilla essence

Cut into squares when cool.

MAKES 30-40 TOFFEES.

Toffee Apples

Wash and dry the apples. Put sugar, water and lemon juice into a saucepan and bring to the boil until the sugar dissolves and mixture becomes pale brown in colour. Remove the saucepan from the heat.

4 eating apples
250 g (8 oz) white sugar
45 ml (1½ fl oz) water
3 tbs lemon juice

Use a fork to skewer the top of each apple and dip the apple into the syrup, making sure it is completely covered.

Leave in a cool place for the syrup to harden.

MAKES 4 TOFFEE APPLES.

Breads,
Pastry, Buns & Scones

Bhatura
Bread Rolls
Brown Bread
Celery Rolls
Cheese Loaf
Chapatis
Cheese Rolls
Corn Bread
Focaccia
Granary Bread
Naan Bread
Toast Sticks
White Bread
Pitta Bread
Puris
Shortbread Pastry

Shortcrust Pastry
Pie Pastry
Chocolate Buns
Crumpets
Jam Buns
Doughnuts
Hot Cross Buns
Apple Scones
Apricot Scones
Banana Scones
Cheese Scones
Fruit Scones
Parsley Scones
Potato Scones
Yoghurt Scones

Bhatura (Opposite)

Mix the flour, salt, sugar, yeast and oil in a bowl. Add yoghurt and water and make into a soft manageable dough. Cover the dough and leave in a warm place for 1-2 hours to rise until double the size. Knead the dough and divide into 6-8 portions. Roll out each portion on a floured surface into 13 cm (5 in) diameter rounds. Heat the oil in a wok. Place the rounds into the hot oil—the bhatura will puff up. Fry on both sides until golden brown. Remove with a draining spoon and place on paper towel to absorb the excess oil.

375 g (12 oz) plain flour
1 tsp salt
1 tbs sugar
1 level tsp instant dried yeast
2 tbs oil
180 ml (6 fl oz) plain yoghurt
4 tbs lukewarm water
oil, for frying

Serve hot with Chick Pea Curry (Channa) (page 53).

MAKES 6-8 BHATURAS.

Bread Rolls

Mix all the dry ingredients together. Add in the water a little at a time to form a soft dough. Cover and leave in a warm place to rise for 1-2 hours. Make into small rolls and allow them to rise until double in size. Once risen, bake in a hot oven at 180°C/350°F/Gas Mark 4 for 20-25 minutes. Brush baked rolls with a little oil.

500 g (1 lb) strong plain flour
1 tsp salt
1 tbs instant dried yeast
600 ml (1 pint) lukewarm water
2 tbs oil

MAKES 10-12 ROLLS.

Brown Bread

Mix the flour and salt in a large bowl. Add sugar and yeast and rub in the butter or margarine. Mix together and add the water slowly to form soft elastic dough. Cover and leave in a warm place to rise for 1-2 hours. Grease a 1 lb loaf tin. Knead the dough and press into the loaf tin. Allow it to rise. Once risen, bake in a hot oven at 180°C/350°F/Gas Mark 4 for 25-30 minutes.

500 g (1 lb) strong wholemeal
bread flour
1 tsp salt
1-2 tbs sugar
30 g (1 oz) instant yeast
30 g (1 oz) butter OR margarine
lukewarm water, to mix

MAKES 1 LOAF.

Celery Rolls

Mix together all the dry dough ingredients and the oil. Add the water a little at a time to form a soft dough. Cover and leave in a warm place to rise for 1-2 hours.

Heat the oil in a pan, add the tomato purée, salt and paprika and cook until the oil has blended into the purée. Leave aside.

Roll out the dough to 5 mm (¼ in) thick and spread the tomato paste evenly all over the dough. Sprinkle cheese and celery evenly over the dough and roll the dough into a Swiss roll. With a knife, cut the rolled dough into 1 cm (½ in) thick slices and place them on a large greased tray, with enough space around them to rise to twice the size. Bake in pre-heated oven at 200°C/400°F/Gas Mark 6 for 20 minutes until brown.

Heat more oil in a small saucepan, add the mustard seeds until they pop, then add the sesame seeds till browned. Spread this over each roll with a teaspoon and sprinkle coriander or parsley on top.

MAKES 6-8 ROLLS.

DOUGH
500 g (1 lb) strong plain flour
1 tsp salt
1 tbs instant dried yeast
2 tbs oil
600 ml (1 pint) lukewarm water
FILLING
185 g (6 oz) tomato purée
2 tbs oil
2 tsp salt
1 tsp paprika
125 g (4 oz) Parmesan cheese, grated
250 g (8 oz) celery, finely chopped
TOPPING
2 tbs oil
1 tsp mustard seeds
2-3 tbs sesame seeds
30 g (1 oz) fresh coriander OR parsley

Cheese Loaf

Heat liquid and oil until lukewarm. Combine flour, yeast, salt and cheese in a large bowl. Add liquid and mix together to form the dough. Knead for 10 minutes, place in a bowl and cover with a damp cloth. Leave in a warm area to rise for 1 hour. Knead again for 10 minutes until the dough is smooth and elastic. Place in a 1 kg (2 lb) loaf tin, cover with a damp cloth and leave to prove in a warm place for 30-40 minutes.

Bake in a hot oven at 220°C/425°F/Gas Mark 7 for 15 minutes, then lower the temperature to 190°C/375°F/Gas Mark 5 for a further 20-25 minutes, until the bread sounds hollow when tapped. Turn onto a wire rack.

The amount of liquid varies according to the type of flour used. Wholegrain flours need more liquid.

MAKES 1 LOAF.

600 ml (1 pint) water OR milk OR
* half water, half milk*
1 tbs oil
500 g (1 lb) bread flour
1 tbs instant dried yeast
¼ tsp salt
60 g (2 oz) strong Cheddar cheese,
* grated*

Chapatis

Put flour in a bowl and rub in the oil. Make a soft dough by adding the water, cover and leave aside for 1 hour.

Place an iron griddle or heavy flat pan on a medium heat. Knead the dough with oiled hands and divide into 20 small portions. Make into balls using the palms of your hands. Flatten the balls and roll out on floured surface into rounds 18 cm (7 in) in diameter.

Place one rolled chapati on the hot griddle or pan. Cook one side, turn after 20-30 seconds and cook the other side. Turn frequently so it doesn't burn. Remove from the pan when puffed up, place on a paper towel on a plate, and lightly spread with butter or margarine.

MAKES 20 CHAPATIS.

375 g (12 oz) chapati flour
1-2 tbs oil
250 ml (8 fl oz) warm water
butter OR margarine

Cheese Rolls

Make the dough as for Cheese Loaf (opposite) and after it has risen the first time, divide it into 10 equal pieces. Knead each piece into a ball and place a teaspoon of Cottage Cheese in centre of each roll. Make sure the cheese is completely sealed in. Place onto a floured baking tray. Cover and leave to rise until doubled in size.

Bake in a hot oven at 220°C/425°F/Gas Mark 7 for 10-15 minutes.

MAKES 10 ROLLS.

2½ tbs Cottage Cheese (page 212)

Corn Bread

Combine milk, oil and molasses in a bowl. Sift the dry ingredients together, then sift again into the liquid ingredients. Mix thoroughly and place the dough in well-greased loaf tin.

Bake at 220°C/425°F/Gas Mark 7 for about 20-30 minutes.

Masa Harina: a corn flour used to make tortillas, available in the baking or Mexican food section of most grocery stores.

SERVES 6.

180 ml (6 fl oz) milk
100 ml (3 fl oz) oil
3 tbs molasses
90 g (3 oz) cornmeal
8 g (¼ oz) masa harina
30 g (1 oz) unbleached white flour
2 tsp baking powder
2 tbs sugar
1 tsp salt

Focaccia (Opposite)

Sift the flour and salt into a fairly large bowl. Add the oil and yeast. Make a soft dough using water. Cover and leave in a warm place to rise. When it has risen, knead the dough again for a couple of minutes and roll it out to 2.5 cm (1 in) thick. Grease a flat baking tray, and place the rolled dough on it. Press fingertips lightly into the dough. Sprinkle on oregano, oil and a little salt.

Bake in a hot oven at 200°C/400°F/Gas Mark 6 for 45 minutes.

Variations: olives and sun dried tomatoes can be mixed into the flour.

MAKES 1 LOAF.

500 g (1 lb) bread flour
1 tsp salt
6 tbs oil
30 g (1 oz) instant dried yeast
360 ml (12 fl oz) lukewarm water, to mix
60 g (2 oz) oregano for topping
oil, for topping
salt, for topping

Granary Bread

Melt the butter or margarine in a saucepan and leave to cool. Place flour, salt, sugar and yeast in a bowl and mix together, then rub in the butter. Add water to form a soft dough. Knead the dough well, cover with a tea towel and leave in a warm place to rise for 45 minutes to 1 hour. Knead again for 5 minutes and put in a greased bread tin. Cover with a tea towel and allow to rise again.

Bake in the centre of a hot oven at 220°C/425°F/Gas Mark 7 for 30-35 minutes. Cool on a wire rack.

MAKES 1 LOAF.

60 g (2 oz) butter OR margarine
500 g (1 lb) granary flour
1 tsp salt
2 tbs brown sugar
30 g (1 oz) instant dried yeast
360 ml (12 fl oz) water

Naan Bread

Place flour, salt, sugar and yeast in a large bowl and mix together. Add yoghurt, water and oil to make a soft dough. Cover the dough with a tea cloth and leave in a warm place to rise until double the size. Knead the dough and divide it into 8 balls. Dip in dry flour and roll out each ball into an oval shape on a floured surface. Heat an iron griddle or a frying pan and cook like a chapati until golden brown.

Serve with any vegetable curry.

MAKES 8 NAANS.

500 g (1 lb) plain flour
1½ tsp salt
1 tsp sugar
1½ level tsp instant dried yeast
180 ml (6 oz) plain yoghurt
125 ml (4 fl oz) water
60 g (2 fl oz) oil
plain flour, for rolling out

Toast Sticks

Mix butter or margarine, sugar, bicarbonate of soda, custard powder and food colouring until soft and fluffy. Add milk, flour, salt and fennel seeds and form into a soft dough. Take small portions of dough and roll between the palms of your hand into long sticks and bake at 180°C/350°F/Gas Mark 4 for 25-30 minutes.

MAKES 12-15 STICKS.

60 g (2 oz) butter OR margarine
3 tsp sugar
pinch of bicarbonate of soda
2 tsp custard powder
2 drops of yellow food colouring (optional)
2-3 tbs milk
250 g (8 oz) plain flour
1 tsp salt
8 g (¼ oz) fennel seeds

White Bread

Sift flour and salt into a large bowl, add sugar and yeast. Mix in the oil and add the water slowly to form soft and elastic dough. Cover and leave in a warm place to rise for 1-2 hours. Grease a 500 g (1 lb) loaf tin. Knead the dough for 5-10 minutes and press into the tins. Leave to rise again. Once risen, bake in a hot oven at 180°C/350°F/Gas Mark 4 for 25-30 minutes.

This recipe can be used to make 12-15 bread rolls.

MAKES 1 LOAF OR 12-15 ROLLS.

500 g (1 lb) strong white bread flour
1 tsp salt
2 tbs oil
1-2 tsp sugar
30 g (1 oz) dried instant yeast
lukewarm water, to mix

Pitta Bread (Opposite)

Sift the flour and salt into a fairly large mixing bowl. Mix in the yeast and sugar. Mix oil, yoghurt and lukewarm water together, then add to the dry ingredients to form the dough. Knead well for 5-7 minutes. Cover and leave in a warm place for 1-2 hours to rise. Turn onto a floured surface and divide into 10-12 portions, depending on the size required. Roll out each portion into an oval shape and place on a heavy flat pan. Cook on both sides over a low heat until browned. Pitta bread should puff up and can be frozen once cold.

Pitta breads are ideal for filling with a salad.

MAKES 10-12 PITTA BREADS.

500 g (1 lb) white bread flour
1 tsp salt
30 g (1 oz) instant dried yeast
1½ tbs sugar
1-2 tsp vegetable oil
2 tbs plain yoghurt
lukewarm water, to mix

Puris

Mix the flour and oil together in a bowl. Pour in the water little by little to make a smooth, firm dough. Knead it for 3-5 minutes and leave it to stand for ½ hour.

Heat the oil in a deep frying pan. Knead the dough again and make small round balls, the size of a walnut. Roll each ball to about 7.5 cm (3 in) in diameter and put into the hot oil. Puris should puff up like a ball. Turn them gently onto the other side and cook for 30 seconds. Place on a paper towel to remove any excess oil.

Can be served hot or cold.

MAKES 30 PURIS.

500 g (1 lb) chapati flour
2-3 tbs oil
lukewarm water, to mix
oil, for frying

Shortbread Pastry

Put the flours, sugar and salt into a bowl. Rub in the butter or margarine to form a breadcrumb texture. Add sufficient cold water to form a fairly soft dough, not too runny, taking care to handle it as little as possible. Leave to rest in the refrigerator for at least 30 minutes.

Roll out to 1 cm (½ in) thick on a well floured surface and fit in a baking tray. Prick the base with a fork and top with a filling.

Bake at 200°C/400°F/Gas Mark 6 for 20 minutes.

750 g (1½ lb) plain flour
315 g (10 oz) self-raising flour
220 g (7 oz) sugar
1 tsp salt
410 g (13 oz) butter OR margarine
water, to mix

Shortcrust Pastry

Sift the flour and salt into a bowl. Add butter or margarine, cut into small pieces. Rub the butter or margarine into the flour with the fingertips until the mixture has the texture of breadcrumbs. Add water and knead the mixture into a pliable dough. Allow to rest in the refrigerator for at least 30 minutes.

Roll out on a well floured surface and use to line a pie dish, put in a filling of your choice and cook at 200°C/400°F/Gas Mark 6 for 20 minutes.

ENOUGH FOR TWO 25 CM (10 IN) PIES.

1 kg (2 lb) plain flour
1 tsp salt
500 g (1 lb) butter OR margarine
180 ml (6 fl oz) cold water

Pie Pastry

Sift the flour into a bowl. Add sugar, butter or margarine and rub into the flour. Add water to form a firm dough. Allow to rest in the refrigerator for at least 30 minutes.

Roll out on a well floured surface and use to line a pie dish, put in a filling of your choice and cook at 200°C/400°F/Gas Mark 6 for 20 minutes.

ENOUGH FOR TWO 25 CM (10 IN) PIES.

500 g (1 lb) plain flour
60 g (2 oz) caster sugar
345 g (11 oz) butter OR margarine
2 tbs water

Chocolate Buns (Opposite)

Sift flour, custard powder and salt into a large bowl. Add the yeast and sugar and mix. Pour milk slowly into the flour to form a soft dough. Cover the bowl and leave in a warm place for 1 hour to rise. Knead the dough for 2-3 minutes and leave to rise again until doubled in size. Divide the dough into 14-16 small balls. Place dough balls on a greased baking tray and cover with a tea cloth. Put in a warm place until they have risen to twice the size.

Bake in a hot oven at 200°C/400°F/Gas Mark 6 for 10-13 minutes until golden brown. Remove and place on a wire rack to cool.

Break the cooking chocolate into small pieces and put in a glass bowl. To melt the chocolate, place the bowl over hot water to melt the chocolate or microwave for 2 minutes. Dip just the top half of the cooled buns into the chocolate.

MAKES 14-16 BUNS.

500 g (1 lb) plain flour
2 tbs custard powder
pinch of salt
30 g (1 oz) dried instant yeast
4 tbs sugar
600 ml (1 pint) lukewarm milk
440 g (14 oz) cooking chocolate

Crumpets

Sift the flour and salt into a bowl. Add yeast and sugar and mix together. Add lukewarm milk to the flour and mix thoroughly until a smooth batter is formed. Cover the bowl with a cloth and leave to stand for 1 hour. Grease a frying pan, placing crumpet rings or pastry cutters on it. When the pan is hot, pour a tablespoon of batter into each ring. Lift off the rings and turn the crumpets over gently. Cook them until golden brown on both sides.

MAKES 12-14 CRUMPETS.

500 g (1 lb) plain flour
1½ tsp salt
2 tbs dried instant yeast
30 g (1 oz) sugar
750 ml (1¼ pints) milk, lukewarm
oil, for frying

Jam Buns

Sift flour and salt in a bowl. Rub the butter or margarine into the flour until the mixture resembles fine breadcrumbs. Add the sugar and milk. Mix to make a stiff dough. Turn out onto a floured board and knead lightly. Divide into small pieces. Make an indent in the middle of each bun and put in ½ teaspoon of jam.

Bake at 220°C/425°F/Gas Mark 7 for 20 minutes.

MAKES 10-12 BUNS.

250 g (8 oz) self-raising flour
pinch of salt
90 g (3 oz) butter OR margarine
125 g (4 oz) sugar
125 ml (4 fl oz) milk
5-6 tsp jam

Doughnuts (Opposite)

Mix together flour, dry yeast, sugar and salt. Add oil and rub in well. Gradually add sufficient water to mix to a firm dough. Knead for about 10 minutes or until smooth. Roll out and cut into rounds and form the hole with your fingers. For oblong doughnuts, divide into 16 pieces and roll into shape. Place doughnuts well apart on an oiled baking tray, and leave in a warm place to rise until double in size. Deep fry over a medium heat for 2 minutes on each side or until golden brown. Dip in a mixture of caster sugar and cinnamon whilst still hot.

MAKES ABOUT 16 DOUGHNUTS.

625 g (1¼ lb) white plain flour
8 g (¼ oz) instant dried yeast
4 tbs sugar
1½ tsp salt
3 tbs oil
420 ml (14 fl oz) warm water
1.2 l (2 pints) oil, for frying
caster sugar, for dusting
pinch of cinnamon, ground for dusting

Hot Cross Buns

Sift the flour and salt into a large bowl. Add sugar and yeast, rub in the butter or margarine and add all the spices and fruits. Mix together and add the water slowly to form a soft elastic dough. Cover and leave in a warm place to rise for 1-2 hours.

Punch down the dough. Divide it into 12-14 pieces, form into balls, and place them 2.5 cm (1 in) apart on a greased baking tray. Cover and put in a warm place for 30 minutes or until well puffed up. Set the oven to 220°C/425°F/Gas Mark 7. Bake for 20 minutes. Heat the sugar and milk or water until the sugar is dissolved, and brush the tops of the buns with it. Cool on a wire rack.

Mix the icing sugar and lemon juice to a paste consistency and make crosses over the buns using an icing bag.

MAKES 12-14 BUNS.

DOUGH
500 g (1 lb) strong white bread flour
1 tsp salt
1-2 tbs sugar
30 g (1 oz) dried instant yeast
30 g (1 oz) butter OR margarine
½ tsp mixed spice
½ tsp cinnamon, ground
½ tsp nutmeg, grated
90 g (3 oz) currants OR sultanas
lukewarm water, to mix
30 g (1 oz) sugar
2 tbs milk

ICING
90 g (3 oz) icing sugar
1 tsp lemon juice

Apple Scones

Sift together the flour, salt and baking powder. Rub in the butter or margarine. Add the sugar, then the apple and enough milk to make a soft, but not sticky, dough. Turn the mixture onto a floured surface and knead lightly. Roll out into a 20 cm (8 in) round and place on a greased and floured baking tray. Mark the scone into 8 pieces. Brush all over the top with milk and sprinkle with demerara sugar if desired.

Bake at 200°C/400°F/Gas Mark 6 for 20-25 minutes or until well risen and golden brown. Remove from the oven and cool for 10 minutes.

MAKES 8 SCONES.

250 g (8 oz) plain flour
½ tsp salt
2 tsp baking powder
60 g (2 oz) butter OR margarine
60 g (2 oz) caster sugar
1 medium size cooking apple, grated
4 tbs milk
milk, for topping
demerara sugar, for topping (optional)

Apricot Scones

Grease and flour two 18 cm (7 in) sandwich tins. Mix all the ingredients thoroughly in a bowl except the milk. Add enough milk to make a soft dough. Divide in half. Roll out each half to about 2.5 cm (1 in) thick and cut 7 scones from each half. Place 7 scones in each sandwich tin, 6 around the edge and one in the middle.

Bake at 200°C/400°F/Gas Mark 6 for 30 minutes.

MAKES 14 SCONES.

500 g (1 lb) self-raising flour
2 tsp salt
30 g (1 oz) caster sugar
315 g (10 oz) butter OR margarine
rind of 1 orange, grated
60 g (2 oz) dried apricots, soaked and chopped
60 g (2 oz) raisins
250 ml (8 fl oz) milk

Banana Scones

Put the flour, baking powder and sugar into a mixing bowl. Rub in the butter or margarine. Stir banana and water into the flour mixture. Knead lightly. Turn the mixture onto a lightly floured surface. Roll out to 2.5 cm (1 in) thick. With a 5 cm (2 in) pastry cutter, stamp out 18 scones. Place scones on greased and floured baking sheets, brush with a little milk and sprinkle with demerara sugar if desired.

Bake at 200°C/400°F/Gas Mark 6 for 15 minutes or until golden brown and firm to touch. Cool on a wire rack.

MAKES 18 SCONES.

220 g (7 oz) plain flour
4 tsp baking powder
60 g (2 oz) caster sugar
90 g (3 oz) butter OR margarine
250 g (8 oz) banana, mashed
150 ml (¼ pint) water
milk, for topping
2 tbs demerara sugar (optional)

Cheese Scones

Place flour and salt in a bowl. Rub butter or margarine into the flour until the mixture resembles fine breadcrumbs. Add the cheese and enough milk and water to make a soft dough. Turn out onto a lightly floured surface and roll out thickly. Slice into 3.5 cm (1½ in) thick rounds. Arrange on the tray, brush the tops with a little milk and bake at 220°C/425°F/Gas Mark 7 for 10-15 minutes or until well risen and golden brown. Cool on a wire rack.

Serve with cream, cream cheese or jam.

MAKES 10-12 SCONES.

250 g (8 oz) self-raising flour
pinch of salt
60 g (2 oz) butter OR margarine
90 g (3 oz) mild Cheddar cheese, grated
150 ml (¼ pint) milk and water mixed

Fruit Scones

Sift flour, baking powder and sugar. Cut the butter or margarine into small pieces and rub into the flour. Add sultanas. Pour in milk and mix to form a soft dough. With a rolling pin, roll out to 1 cm (½ in) thick and cut with a scone cutter.

Bake at 220°C/425°F/Gas Mark 7 for 12-15 minutes.

Standard Scone Mix is butter rubbed into flour and a pinch of salt.

MAKES 10-12 SCONES.

250 g (8 oz) self-raising flour
1 tsp baking powder
30 g (1 oz) caster sugar
60 g (2 oz) butter OR margarine
125 g (4 oz) sultanas
7 tbs milk

Parsley Scones

Mix thoroughly all ingredients except 30 g (1 oz) of cheese and the milk. Add enough milk to mix to a soft dough. Cut dough in half and shape each half into a 15 cm (6 in) round. Place on two floured baking sheets. Mark each round into 6 wedges, cutting nearly halfway through the dough. Brush the tops with milk and sprinkle the remaining cheese over.

Bake at 200°C/400°F/Gas Mark 6 for 30 minutes.

MAKES 12 SCONES.

500 g (1 lb) self-raising flour
¼ tsp cayenne pepper
2 tbs fresh parsley, chopped
315 g (10 oz) butter OR margarine
pinch of salt
220 g (7 oz) mature Cheddar cheese, grated
250 ml (8 fl oz) milk
milk, for glazing

Potato Scones

Set oven to 220°C/425°F/Gas Mark 7. Sift flour, baking powder and salt into a bowl and mix with butter or margarine and potatoes. Add sufficient milk to form a soft dough. Turn out onto a floured surface and knead lightly. Roll out to 1 cm (½ in) thick and cut into small triangles. Place the scones on a floured baking sheet. Brush each scone with milk. Bake for 10-15 minutes until golden brown.

MAKES 6-8 SCONES.

250 g (8 oz) self-raising flour
1 tsp baking powder
¼ tsp salt
60 g (2 oz) butter OR margarine
60 g (2 oz) potatoes, boiled, peeled and mashed
4 tbs milk

Yoghurt Scones

Set the oven to 220°C/425°F/Gas Mark 7. Sift flour, salt and baking powder into a bowl. Rub in the butter or margarine until the mixture resembles breadcrumbs, then stir in the sugar. Add yoghurt and mix to a soft dough. Knead very gently on a floured surface and roll out to 1 cm (½ in) thick. Cut into small rounds with a cutter and place on floured baking sheets. Bake for 12-15 minutes. Cool on a wire rack.

For best results, don't handle the dough too much.

Variation: add 1 teaspoon of dry mustard and a pinch of cayenne pepper to the dry ingredients. Replace the sugar with 90 g (3 oz) grated cheese and 1 tablespoon of sesame seeds.

Eat them on the day they are made.

MAKES 12-15 SCONES.

250 g (8 oz) wholemeal flour
½ tsp salt
½ tsp baking powder
60 g (2 oz) butter OR margarine
1 tbs muscovado sugar
150 ml (¼ pint) plain yoghurt

Drinks

Banana Milk Shake
Coconut and Banana Shake
Elderflower Cordial
Fresh Lemonade
Fruit and Vegetable Drink
Fruit Cocktail
Pineapple Nectar
Mango Milk Shake

Banana Milk Shake

Liquidise all the ingredients in a blender and serve chilled.

SERVES 1-2.

1 banana, sliced
500 ml (½ pint) milk
1 tbs honey OR sugar

Coconut and Banana Shake

Blend all the ingredients, except the coconut, in a blender for about 1 minute. Pour into a glass and sprinkle the coconut on top.

SERVES 3-4.

250 ml (8 oz) plain yoghurt
1 banana, sliced
1 tsp honey
2-3 drops vanilla essence
1 tsp desiccated coconut

Elderflower Cordial

Pour all the ingredients into a bucket. Stir until the sugar is dissolved. Leave for 24 hours, then strain carefully. The syrup can be frozen. Ice cube bags are ideal as 1 cube is enough for a tumbler of drink. To drink, dilute to taste with water.

SERVES 6-8.

25 elderflower heads
60 g (2 oz) citric acid
2 chopped lemons
1 kg (2 lb) caster sugar
1.2 l (2 pints) boiling water

Fresh Lemonade (Opposite)

Peel lemon finely and squeeze out the juice. Dissolve honey or sugar in water, add lemon peel and let stand for 30 minutes. Then add the lemon juice. Chill. Strain before serving.

SERVES 4-6.

1 lemon
honey OR sugar to taste
600 ml (1 pint) boiling water

Fruit and Vegetable Drink

Liquidise the juices and cucumber together in a blender. Decorate with mint.

SERVES 6-8.

125 ml (4 fl oz) carrot juice
125 ml (4 fl oz) orange juice
250 ml (8 fl oz) apple juice
¼ cucumber, peeled
mint, for decoration

Fruit Cocktail

Mix all the juices. Add lime to taste. Garnish with small chunks of fresh fruit. Serve chilled.

Suggested fruits for garnishing are pineapple, nectarine, peach, orange, kiwi.

SERVES 25-30.

2.1 l (3½ pints) red grape juice
2.1 l (3½ pints) pineapple juice
3.15 l (5¼ pints) orange juice
limes, freshly squeezed
fresh fruit, for garnish

Pineapple Nectar

Place yoghurt, pineapple juice and honey or sugar in a blender and blend. Serve chilled, decorated with fresh pineapple cubes and sprinkled with coconut.

SERVES 6.

125 ml (4 oz) plain yoghurt
125 ml (4 fl oz) pineapple juice
1 tbs honey OR sugar
fresh pineapple, cubed for decoration
desiccated coconut, for decoration

Mango Milk Shake (Opposite)

Place all the ingredients in a blender and blend until soft and creamy. Serve chilled.

Variation: *Strawberry Milk Shake* **can be made using 250 g (8 oz) of strawberries instead of mangoes and 1-2 teaspoons of sugar.**

SERVES 4.

600 ml (1 pint) milk
2 large ripe mangoes, peeled and chopped
1 tsp sugar

Jams,
Cheese
& Yoghurt

Date Spread
Mincemeat—Sugarless
Mincemeat—Preserve
Blackberry and Apple Jam
Raspberry and Rhubarb Jam
Green Tomato and Apple Jam
Orange Marmalade
Orange and Carrot Jam
Strawberry Jam
Dried Apricot Jam
Paneer
Cottage Cheese
Yoghurt

Tips for preparing and preserving jams

1) FRUITS

Fresh, dry and not over-ripe.

2) SUGAR

Preserving OR granulated sugar.

3) PROPORTION

1 part of Fruit to 1 part of Sugar.

4) COOKING

Use a preserving pan (a thick-based saucepan) and fill no more than two-thirds. Use a wooden spoon to stir jam.
Sugar must not be allowed to boil until it has dissolved. Jam should boil steadily. Marmalade should boil gently.

5) TO TEST FOR SETTING POINT

When the jam has been boiling for 5 minutes, remove the pan from the heat and spoon a little onto an ice-cold saucer, before adding the sugar. Leave in the refrigerator until cold. If the surface of the jam frills and wrinkles when pushed with the finger, the jam is at setting point. If not, return the pan to the heat and boil for a further 3-5 minutes. Test again as before. Repeat until setting point is reached.

6) JARS

Clean, dry, warm glass or earthenware jars should be used.

7) COVERING AND LABELLING

It can be done immediately, or when the jam is cold (in which case a teaspoon of vinegar on top will stop the jam from going mouldy). Use wax tissue or cellophane paper.

Date Spread

Remove any stones or stems from the dates, and chop them. Cook the dates gently with water in a saucepan until soft. Add the lemon juice. After cooking, store in a jar in the refrigerator.

250 g (8 oz) dates
300 ml (½ pint) water
1 tsp lemon juice

Mincemeat–Sugarless

Stir all the ingredients together well. Mix at least a day before needed, and stir from time to time.

This mincemeat should not be kept for more than a week, as it contains no sugar.

250 g (8 oz) currants
125 g (4 oz) seeded raisins, chopped
125 g (4 oz) sultanas
375 g (12 oz) Bramley apples, unpeeled, cored and grated
1 tsp orange peel, grated
1 tsp mixed spice
3 tbs lemon juice
2 tbs oil

Mincemeat–Preserve

Wash the dried fruit. Mix the mixed spice and lemon rind with the sugar. Add the dried fruit, lemon juice, fat or oil, apples and mixed peel. Stir well. Allow to stand for at least one day before use, stirring from time to time. Keep covered to prevent drying out.

This mincemeat can be put in jars and will keep for weeks.

MAKES AT LEAST 72 MINCE PIES.

250 g (8 oz) currants
250 g (8 oz) sultanas
1¼ tsp mixed spice
juice and rind of 1 lemon
500 g (1 lb) sugar
185 g (6 oz) vegetable fat OR 180 ml (6 fl oz) oil
250 g (8 oz) Bramley apples, unpeeled, cored and grated
125 g (4 oz) mixed peel

Blackberry and Apple Jam

Stew the apples and blackberries in a pan, then mash them to a pulp. Add the sugar, heat gently until dissolved, then boil rapidly until setting point is reached. Skim, pour into warm, dry jars and cover.

MAKES 2.5 KG (5 LB).

375 g (12 oz) cooking apples, peeled, cored and sliced
300 ml (½ pint) water
1 kg (2 lb) blackberries
1.5 kg (3 lb) preserving sugar

Raspberry and Rhubarb Jam

Wash, peel (if necessary) and cut up the rhubarb. Stew it gently in the water until reduced to a thick pulp. Whilst it stews, wash the raspberries and add them to the rhubarb. Add the sugar. Cook over a low heat, stirring constantly, until the sugar dissolves. Bring to the boil, and then boil rapidly until setting point is reached. Skim and pour the jam into clean, warm jam jars and cover.

MAKES 2.5 KG (5 LB).

1 kg (2 lb) rhubarb
500 g (1 lb) raspberries
1.5 kg (3 lb) preserving sugar
150 ml (¼ pint) water

Green Tomato and Apple Jam (Opposite)

Thinly slice the tomatoes. Peel, core and chop the apples. Put all the ingredients into a large pan, mix well and leave for 1-2 days until it becomes a syrupy mass. Put over a low heat until the sugar is dissolved, then boil rapidly until setting point is reached. Pour into hot sterilised jars and cover tightly. Keep for a few weeks before eating.

500 g (1 lb) green tomatoes
500 g (1 lb) cooking apples
625 g (1¼ lb) granulated sugar
2 tbs vinegar, cider or malt
2 tbs water

Tip: use some of the sugar to cover the cut tomatoes whilst cutting up the apples. To stop them from going brown, cover the apples too, as they go in with the tomatoes.

MAKES ABOUT 1.25 KG (2½ LB).

Orange Marmalade (Opposite)

Scrub and halve the oranges, squeeze the juice into a large saucepan and add the lemon juice. Slice the orange peel into long thin slices. Add the peel and the water to the large saucepan. Bring to the boil, reduce heat and cook slowly for about 2 hours until the peel is soft. It should squash easily between the fingers and the liquid should be well reduced. Add sugar and stir until dissolved—do not allow it to boil at this stage. Increase the heat and bring to a full boil for about 15 minutes. Remove from the heat and test. If the setting point has been reached then add the butter and leave the marmalade to stand for 15 minutes. Stir, to distribute the peel. Leave to cool before putting into jars.

MAKES 3.5 KG (7 LB).

1.75 kg (3½ lb) Seville oranges
6 tsp lemon juice
3.6 l (6 pints) water
3 kg (6 lb) preserving sugar
1 tsp butter

Orange and Carrot Jam

Peel the oranges. Wash and finely shred the orange peel. Place in a preserving pan or thick-based saucepan with half of the water. Bring to the boil, strain and throw this water away. Put the oranges back into the pan with the second half of the water. Bring to the boil for 10 minutes. Add the carrots and cook for a further 10-15 minutes. If it dries, add more water. Add sugar and boil at a high temperature, stirring often with a wooden spoon, until the consistency is like syrup. Add butter and lemon juice, and stir. Leave to cool and, whilst still warm, put into sterilised jars and seal them.

MAKES 2 KG (4 LB) OF JAM.

1 kg (2 lb) oranges, skinned
1 l (1¾ pints) water
500 g (1 lb) carrot, grated
500 g (1 lb) preserving sugar
2 tsp butter
juice of ½ lemon

Strawberry Jam (Opposite)

Put the strawberries into a heavy pan and cook for 5 minutes, stirring occasionally until they are soft and pulpy. Add sugar and lemon juice. Stir over a low heat until the sugar is dissolved. Increase the heat and boil rapidly until setting point is reached. Put into jam jars and cover.

2.5 g (5 lb) strawberries
1 kg (2 lb) preserving sugar
juice of 1 lemon

MAKES 2.5 KG (5 LB).

Dried Apricot Jam

Wash the apricots under cold running water. Place them in a large mixing bowl and pour the water over. Leave to soak overnight. Next day, put the apricots and water into a large pan and add lemon juice. Cover with a lid and simmer for 30 minutes until tender. Remove the lid and boil rapidly until the contents have reduced by about a third. Remove the pan from the heat and stir in the sugar. Return to a low heat and stir until the sugar has dissolved. Raise the heat and boil for a further 5 minutes, then test again. Stir in the butter to reduce the scum, then cool for 15 minutes. Pour the jam into clean, warm jam jars. Immediately press a waxed disc onto the surface. Leave to cool, then cover with cellophane. Label with name and date.

500 g (1 lb) dried apricots, quartered
1.8 l (3 pints) cold water
juice of 2 large lemons
1.5 kg (3 lb) granulated sugar
1 tsp butter

MAKES 2 KG (4 LB).

Paneer

Heat the milk to boiling point, then add the lemon juice or vinegar, and the yoghurt. As it starts to separate, lower the heat to medium for 1-2 minutes and then take the pan off the heat. Strain through a large sieve or cheesecloth. If cheesecloth is used, gather the paneer in the centre, tie a knot and put it on a flat surface. To drain off the excess water, place a heavy object, such as a large pan filled with water, on top. Cut into cubes.

The water from the paneer can be used for soups. Paneer can be frozen.

600 ml (1 pint) milk
juice of 1 lemon OR ¼ tsp cider vinegar
5-6 tbs plain yoghurt

Cottage Cheese

Crumble the cold paneer and add 3-4 tablespoons of plain yoghurt.

Cottage Cheese will last for a week in the refrigerator.

Finely chop cucumber, tomato and fresh parsley. Mix with paneer, salt, pepper and cumin seeds or fennel seeds. Serve on toast or as toasted sandwiches.

Paneer
3-4 tbs plain yoghurt

Yoghurt

Bring the milk to the boil in a pan. Leave to cool until just lukewarm. Mix a little of the warm milk with the yoghurt. When smooth, add to the rest of the warm milk. For the yoghurt to thicken, either pour it into a vacuum flask and leave to stand overnight or pour it into a small glass or steel bowl, cover with a lid and leave to stand in a moderately warm place for 6-8 hours (or overnight).

Yoghurt can be kept for up to 5 days in a refrigerator.

MAKES 600 ML (1 PINT).

600 ml (1 pint) milk
1 tbs plain yoghurt

Inspiration from the Brahma Kumaris

Code 7230 • Paperback • $6.95

From Dadi Janki's lifelong pursuit of developing an internal sense of the Divine, and sharing that experience with the world, she developed *Pearls of Wisdom*. Each inspiring thought is set on its own page for easy reading, understanding and enjoyment.

Code 8385 • Paperback • $8.95

Blessings are simple yet heartfelt messages inspired by the teachings of Raja Yoga, a centuries-old study that cultivates self-reliance, spirituality, and value-based living. Divided into themes on love, success, adversity, friendship and others, each page offers an uplifting message that will empower, comfort, or motivate. *Eternal Blessings* will remind spouses that they are loved, cheer up coworkers on challenging days, and comfort friends in difficult times.

Code 6722 • Paperback • $10.95

Wings of Soul provides you with the tools you need to remove mental and emotional obstacles to self-fulfillment. Dadi shows how every one of us can find our spiritual identity and make a very practical contribution to a better life and a better world.

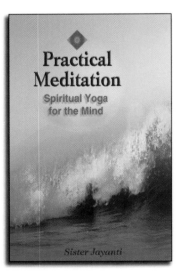

Code 827X • Paperback • $10.95

In every corner of the world people are searching for ways to develop tolerance, balance and power over their thoughts. *Practical Meditation* is an essential compilation of inspirational passages, exercises and mantras that will bring you a sense of clarity, self-awareness and peace of mind.